WHAT THIS MEANS TO YOU

A MILLENNIAL'S TAKE
ON GETTING AHEAD

WHAT THIS MEANS TO YOU

A MILLENNIAL'S TAKE ON GETTING AHEAD

Written by
JOSH CALCANIS

(C) 2016 by Josh Calcanis.

Published by **MERAKI HOUSE PUBLISHING INC.**

All rights reserved. This book or any portion thereof may not be reproduced or used in any manner whatsoever without the express written permission of the publisher except for the use of brief quotations in a book review.

For any information regarding permission contact Josh Calcanis via

WWW.JOSHCALCANIS.COM

Printed in the United States of America
First publication, 2016.

Paperback ISBN - 978-0-9937996-9-3

Book cover design by

CONTENTS

Dedication	vii
Acknowledgements	vix
Foreword	11
Prologue – I'm a Sales Guy	13
Put Your Heart into It	19
Step Out of the Tunnel	31
Be an Exceptional Communicator	41
Live Fearlessly	51
There is No "I" in Team… Really Though	59
The Fall of Financial Literacy	69
The 9 to 5 Millionaire	79
Do Something Nice Without Getting Caught	87
Thank You??	97
Rejection Won't Kill You	105
The Daily Goal	113
Excuse Me Sir, I'm Different	123
Ignore the White Noise	131
Success Apathy	139

Action Speaks Louder than Words	147
The Double-Edged Sword	155
Personal Development Builds Net Worth	163
Y.O.L.O. (You Only Live Once)	171
Not Everyone Drinks the Same Cup Of Tea	179
Drop the Velvet Hammer	187
Do A Double Take	195
What Are You Worth	203
Don't Go Invisible	211
Max Out Your Mental 401k	219
Justify Being A Risk-Taker	227
Transparency Gains Trust	235
Plan B Was Created For A Reason	243
Alone Time is More than Just A Spa Day	253
Take Control of Your Ship… You're the Captain	261
Dreams Don't Have an Expiration Date	265
What the Future Means to You	270
Author's Bio	273

DEDICATION

Throughout most of our lives, there are people that stay and go. Those that hurt and empower. The ones that teach us the greatest lessons and those who we can count on for anything. We ALL have those people that are our foundation. Our rock in the tough times. The ones we would trust our lives with if it came down to it. While we haven't always seen eye to eye and I can be a pain in the ass, my family have always been my rock in the toughest of times, and I can't express enough appreciation or love.

Dad, thank you for being my father and for always being as real with me as possible. I've become the man I am today because you raised me. You sacrificed so much to make sure I grew up with an opportunity to do great things. Without your unconditional and (occasionally) tough love, I know I wouldn't be where I am today. You've put things on the back burner to make sure that I could excel. We've fought and argued, but what Greek and Italian family hasn't? If I can raise my children with as much love and guidance that you did with me, then I'll consider myself successful. Thank you for always believing in me, even when I didn't. I love you.

Mom, please don't call the office if I don't text back within an hour. I promise I'm still alive and just haven't had time to grab my phone. In all seriousness, you have taught me to love unconditionally and, most importantly, to forgive. You call, text, email, send smoke signals, and have even called the receptionist at the office to check on me. So much of this is just because you love your two boys more than anything in this world. Caleb and I were never easy, and, no matter what, it always came back to believing in what you thought was right and making sure we knew we were supported and safe. In the end, you showed us love that only a mother could show. The unconditional love that only Mother Teresa could rival. You are the support system that Caleb and I have always (and will always) counted on. You are the voice that will back us up, support us, and protect us no matter what anyone else says about you. I hope I am as strong as you when I have that responsibility. Thank you, and I love you.

Caleb, I'm pretty sure the big brother is supposed to teach you some things, but you've turned that notion upside down. I know you've been through so much these past couple of years, and I've been gone. I've been all over the United States while you were at home fighting your battle. No matter when I came back and visited, you still treated me with the same love and respect any brother would show. You proved to me that blood is thicker than anything else and that is something no one else could have taught me. I love you like a brother (mostly because you are mine) and can't wait to grow older with you. Thank you for always fighting, believing in your big brother, and showing me what unconditional love is all about. You've always got a big brother here for you if you ever need anything.

This book is dedicated to you. My family. The ones who have been there since the beginning and who will always be there for me. I love you all and will never be able to show ALL the appreciation and love you truly deserve, but I'll try my best.

.

ACKNOWLEDGMENTS

Very rarely is an idea brought to fruition without the support of mentors, friends, and family. This is my sincerest thank you for the constant faith in me. I could easily take up another book this size in just acknowledgments alone, but I'll try to keep it shorter.

My first acknowledgment is for my family. They are the reason I'm where I am today and why I continue to push through life with the idea that my life has a greater purpose. I believe I have a purpose in this life and will do something great because that's how I was raised. Each of you brought something unique to my life and made my childhood, adolescent, and adult life something to be grateful for. Thank you.

Something that has always held a significant role in my life was my closest friends. To the crew I grew up with in Sanford (you know who you are), you gave me a bar to judge all other friendships on. You all were part of the most crucial memories and experiences I had in my life all the way through college and still continue to impact me to this day. Thank you for dealing with me for far longer than I'd imagine you would. It didn't stop in Sanford though. Moving three times in four years can make life challenging if you don't have some local support system and a group of friends you can count on. To my Seattle, Los Angeles, and Savannah crew, thank you. Thank you for bringing me in and allowing me to find a family away from home. And dealing with most raw text strings.

Thank you to my coaches and leaders in my life. In college, high school, sports, and any other activity where someone must stand as a leader, I've been lucky. I've had support from numerous people that have made me stronger and better. A big thank you to all those that have been around me during my short career in sales. A lot of the things I've learned (some of it being expressed in this book) have come from you all.

A book doesn't get some attention without an excellent publishing house and fearless leader. Thank you to Meraki House Publishing for making this book a reality and supporting me every step of the way. Thank you to Marnie, who personally takes an interest in every book and author Meraki begins to work with. Your insight is invaluable, and I look forward to working with you and Meraki more in the future.

Thank you to the authors who have expedited my personal development by sharing their expertise and knowledge. Although there are hundreds of books I've stuck my nose into, I want to thank particularly Jeb Blount, who not only gave me advice before finding Meraki House Publishing but also took the time to write my foreword. I appreciate the inspiration and support. Also thank you to Hal Elrod, Rhonda Byrne, Benjamin Graham, Brandon Turner, M.J. DeMarco, Robert Kiyosaki, Sharon Lechter, Jeb Blount, and Daniel Pink. All authors of some of the most impactful reading out there.

Finally, thank you to all those who took a vested interest in your personal growth and read this book. Thank you for the support and just picking up this book. I sincerely hope it impacted just one day or moment in your life for the short 30 days spent reading.

FOREWORD

When I first met Josh he was a student in the Professional Selling Program at the University of Central Florida. The program was packed full of elite students but even among the brightest of the bright, Josh's star shined brilliantly. His optimism, drive, and insatiable desire for success stood out.

Josh learned along the way that talent is never enough because life is a hard grader. It doesn't care about where you went to school, how smart you are, your grades, skills, experience, or your pedigree. Life only rewards those who are willing to work hard, sacrifice, and leverage its lessons to learn and grow.

It's these lessons that inspired this one of a kind book that is devoted to helping you take small daily steps to success. Inside you'll learn that one of the real keys to being healthy, happy, to great relationships, and success in every part of your life, is making this daily investment in yourself.

I've always been a believer in doing a little bit every day to develop and grow. I believe that most great accomplishments are achieved through a series of small steps. With the discipline to do just a little bit every day you can change the trajectory of your life and career.

In What This Means To You Josh shows you the power of daily focus and how it adds up to huge gains in the long-term. He challenges you to turn each day of your life into a valuable learning experience and starts you down that path with 30 unique lessons along with follow up questions that provoke you to move out of your comfort zone and shift your mindset.

I encourage you to take this 30-day challenge. If you do I guarantee you'll find the success deserve.

Jeb Blount

Author of the #1 bestsellers, Fanatical Prospecting and People Buy You

PROLOGUE

I'M A SALES GUY

Let me get the awkward opinion out the way immediately. I'm a salesperson. EWW. Nasty. Try to hold back that dry heave and that image that just popped up of the shady car salesperson. I promise I'm not going to aggressively push the next shake weight on you. Before I got into sales, I felt the same way. I fortunately realized, like any stereotype, there is a big difference in the perception of and who a salesperson really is.

So let me start over… I'm not a millionaire. I'm not an inventor. And I'm not a professional athlete (although my flag football team would beg to differ). Because of those reasons, it's going to be hard for you not to connect with the content in this book. Just because I was the normal 20-something, didn't mean life wasn't throwing lessons my way and create who I've become just like EVERYONE else in this world.

My name is Joshua Calcanis, and I'm a career sales professional. I was the kid in the family that always was told "you'd be great in sales!" It was always after a fundraiser or some event I ended up pulling in more money than everyone else. I always brushed it off. I never really thought of sales as a career and it was because of the negative image I had of sales people. So I just continued to do what I would in every interaction I thought was the norm.

I'd listen, create a logical response, and spit out the answer with more excitement and enthusiasm than someone of any rational thought could say "no" to. I didn't tie that ability to a sales profession until I had begun looking for a job. When I had started to search and started spending time with sales professionals, I realized a lot of the people in my life that had constantly reminded me about sales as a career, were right. I had the natural ability, and my skills just really needed to be polished and perfected. Without much hesitation, I dove into my first professional sales job.

So what's the big difference between a salesperson and a "sales professional"? Simple: the way one looks at communication with a potential buyer. As a sales professional, you're looking at a client's needs and how the product or service you're selling is going to benefit them. Essentially, what a particular feature MEANS to the customer. In this case, you're the eager motivated buyer, and the only thing you're actually 'buying' into is the impact this book will have on your daily life.

Those in sales that can effectively communicate what a feature means to a customer are the ones that succeed in sales and retain an excellent reputation. They are the people who give salespeople the right image I have burned into my mind and hopefully the one you'll have. I'm not going to lie and say I knew I was going to become a sales professional, it just happened. After graduating college, I found myself in a sales job and got hooked. I spent the next five years LIVING.

By that I mean I was working an insane amount of hours during the week, spent time traveling for a job, and spent days developing myself. A common cliché here is the good ole saying "work hard, play hard." Life taught me lessons that I couldn't learn in a classroom, and, fortunately for me, I wrote them down in a journal. I documented a lot of things from middle school to the present day and continued to do so.

After writing one night, I realized that I had become the young man I am today because of my experiences and lessons life so gratuitously shared. That's when it hit me…why can't I share this? Why can't I impact those that are facing these same issues? Millions of people every day run into the same problems, experiences, and life lessons without so much as a warning. I want to change that. As a salesperson, all I needed to do was tell a story, share the lesson, and communicate exactly what that story meant to YOU by doing what I was good at.

What I realized in my 20s was that life is the greatest teacher you can find. Life tends to make use of your youthful ignorance and teach you with heartbreak, embarrassment, and a little modesty. I've experienced these through stepping outside my comfort zone to present in front of a room full of physicians (and was quickly reminded I wasn't the smartest in the room) to something as simple as learning the stock market is not something to play with if you don't know what you're doing. I'm just like you! Everyone goes through this no matter their upbringing or status; it's just the ones that take the lessons they're given and use them to their advantage.

Like I said, I'm no millionaire, I'm not famous, and I haven't created the next big thing, and that's exactly why I know this will be a different book from anything else you've read. These are lessons and experiences that we both can relate to, and together we can decipher the instructions life is throwing our way.

With the stories in this book, you'll have the opportunity to challenge yourself every single day (especially if you read a chapter a day) and FEEL the difference in your life. I want you to use this book to your advantage. I want you to take it as motivation and as a reminder that every situation we face can teach us a valuable lesson. A lesson that can stick with you for the rest of your life or one you can waste. Fortunately, you wouldn't be looking through a book like this unless you were interested in personal development and reaching the best you!

This book is a compilation of stories from my 20s, each ending with the lesson I learned and how you can learn from that lesson as well. These stories are interactions with business professionals, random strangers, and personal friends that, through some exchange, I learned something from, which impacts my daily life today. There is 30 days' worth of life lessons in this book. 30 days to read, change the way you look at each day, and, hopefully, change the way you look at certain situations in the life of an everyday person on the way to everyday greatness.

I challenge you to take your time and read one chapter a day and then actually think about the questions at the end of the chapter. Remember to mark the day you read the chapter and put the questions and lesson into play. Only then should you come back to the last question and answer what that experience meant to you. You'll be able to impact your life in a different way every day for 30 days! When you're done, you can pass this book along to affect someone else's life or run through it again and spend extra time on one experience you want to improve. Whatever you choose, just understand that you and I have a shared goal: by the end of this book, you'll be able to look at the cover and tell everyone what this book meant to you and how it impacted your day-to-day.

DAY 1

- PUT YOUR HEART INTO IT -

With my junior year of college coming to a close, I started to develop SPD; Senior Panic Disorder was a common disease plaguing most graduating seniors in college. At its core, was the deadline all seniors were faced with and one that started to loom over unsuspecting seniors by the end of their junior year. It was time to find a job!

To avoid causing a real panic attack (and to add the disclaimer in here that I'm just a marketing major), SPD is not an actual disorder, but it sure feels like one. I needed to find a way to stand out and get in front of certain employers, so I could start making a living when I graduated. Fortunately for me and all other marketing students, there was a program designed to educate us in the ways of a sales professional. I made it into that program and found out what I had signed up for was more than just another class. During my final semester in college, I learned one of the most valuable lessons I picked up in college from the person who'd hire me.

The spring semester had brought multiple employers, guest speakers, and plenty of motivational emails regarding personal resilience. This semester was all about meeting your future employer, and it was no different for me. I still remember meeting him for the first time in class when he came to introduce himself and his company. He was always candid and confident, but damn could he sell. This energetic and incredibly inspirational man was known as Jason Bristol. I was 21 and member to a select group of marketing students called the Professional Selling Program at the University of Central Florida. This program was comprised of 30 students committed to work and train harder than all other students their senior year of college to graduate with a job paying close to six figures in sales. That is something that was unheard of for college graduates, but so was this intense, real-world driven program.

I mean what other college senior was waking up before 11:00 a.m. on a weekday? I sure wouldn't have if it weren't for this class. Of course, this is a perfect example of why there was such a difference in the those getting jobs out of colleges and those still on the search.

At the end of each semester, the entire class had multiple opportunities to interview with sales companies that were all interested in hiring out of our program. One company, which Jason worked with, was a leader in the medical industry and had grown exponentially since their start-up just a few years earlier. Most businesses that recruited out of our program were Fortune 500 companies or had been around for years. Jason's was a much smaller, private company spearheading a new industry. Still, Jason carried a passion that was not present with any other company that tried to recruit us, which is why so many of us chose to sign up for his cause or, at least, sign up for an interview.

When Jason showed up to interview those interested in the company, he gave one more quick pitch on what this company was really about and how tough this industry was. The class of super students brushed off his warning as if it was another exam and almost the entire class volunteered to the verbal abuse of an interview.

After the interviews, students returned with mixed emotions. Some were still upset, even crying, while others were overwhelmingly jovial. You don't think everyone comes out of an interview happy do you??

Now only one person stood out with a surprisingly unsettled look… it was Jason. He took the final minutes to describe why he looked more thwarted than the guy that just got rejected by the freshman girl. The closing moments with our class were incredibly humbling and something we all needed. Our arrogance as an elite class had started to take hold. He stated that we aced the interview questions and that we all looked great on paper because of the program. It was how we were perceived in the discussions that took the greatest toll…we simply didn't show enough "heart." We acted as if we were entitled to a job instead of having to work for it. We were acting like the spoiled kid in elementary school that felt entitled to the first place in line. Our answers lacked any passion or excitement. We were informed that we had all come off as robotic students created in a lab, which we were in a way, and trained to beat interviews and get a job.

To have someone declare that this unique group of students, bred to surpass quotas and contest rejection, didn't show enough "heart" wasn't the expectation of this goodbye speech. I can also attest that it certainly didn't create any fans in the audience. Of course, that wasn't the point, and Jason was not there just to make friends with students. He was there to teach a lesson, help us grow, and recruit the next set of sales pros. He simply drilled home the fact that if you want something that you have got to show some "heart."

What this experience did was change the way I looked at every encounter, job, and activity. I know why I'm waking up in the morning and make sure to carry that with me throughout the day. If I actively keep in mind what motivates me, putting all my heart into everything becomes natural. Why? Because everything I do, after I remind myself what is motivating me, has a purpose! When you do something that has a purpose and you're giving every action all your heart, like Jason exclaimed, your enthusiasm and excitement radiates off of you whether you like it or not. It's infectious. You can literally feel it when someone is giving everything all their heart!

This isn't just a kid hopped up on "happy" talk here either. There are studies of happiness that show that people feel at their peak (an emotion that psychologists call "flow") when they are engaged in something they find absorbing, challenging, and compelling, especially something that makes a contribution. Stanford professor, William Damon, reports a lot of this research in his book, *The Path to Purpose,* which discusses that the engagement mentioned above is passion and heart that Jason was trying to express to our young class of students.

SO WHAT DOES THIS MEAN TO YOU?

No matter your goals, hopes, or dreams, we all share one common truth. There is always someone amidst the crowd that is working harder than you. With that evident fact, the way to gain the edge on the competition and differentiate yourself is to develop your "heart." No, I don't mean you need any more cardio.

I mean can you look in the mirror and say you give all your heart in everything you do? If not, you've got to find the purpose that will allow you to give all your heart. You've got to understand what wakes you up in the morning and why you continue to do what you do each day! Without it, everyday will be like the interviews above that I did not succeed at. Interactions will be robotic, and life just won't be as lively! My excitement didn't shine through, and Jason made this apparent because I was just going through the motions without understanding what I was doing all that work for!

For example, I wake up now and know why. I have big picture goals (which we'll talk about) looming in the back of mind every day (like positively impacting people around me). That means for everything I do, every action I take, I have a purpose that set's a motivational fire for me and allows me to connect my "heart" to the work I do and the life I live. Think about what motivates you and what could start that everlasting fire in you so that you can use it to give all your heart in everything you do.

Why do you spend your day doing what you do? Use that answer in the way you approach interviews, answer questions, sell, or just approach your next day. By developing your "heart" you create an energy and passion that is powerful. It radiates off of you. Have you ever met someone that just seems like they're happy all the time? They understand what motivates them, and they let it shine through 24/7. It can impact your next conversation in a way you thought only caffeine could.

Who wouldn't want to feel passionate and excited about everything they are doing in their daily lives? Recognize what's in your heart and use it as a fire today!

DAY 1 Completed: ____/____/_____

What is your "heart"/motivation/the reason you wake up?!

Is that something you can see changing in the future? Why?

Why do you think you woke up this morning?

Are those two the same? Why or why not?

How did you use it to motivate you today? How are you going to in the future?

What did this mean to you?

"Wherever you go, go with all your heart"

-Confucius

DAY 2

- STEP OUT OF THE TUNNEL -

With my collegiate career coming to an end, the opportunity to share what I had learned in the Professional Selling Program presented itself in the form of a final presentation. The guidelines were simple: take up an absurd amount of time and slowly lull the audience into REM sleep. It's as if we were graded on how much drool we could force from our audience's mouth than anything else. Fortunately, I teamed up with someone who decided to stray from the guidelines in search of a more "exciting" presentation. While we managed to keep everyone awake with a stellar performance, my priority was to mention that the most eloquent message I received that year was from a friend of mine that I had unintentionally offended just a few months prior.

The spring semester in the UCF Professional Selling Program is ultimately a marathon of competition. As someone who hates to lose, the semester sent me through a roller coaster of emotion in search for every possible win. It was the last semester and as a Portland local looking for their next Prius, nothing was going to stand in my way of graduating this program and getting a well-paying job. Slowly, I began to lose sight of what was important and had become consumed by the work I was doing—commonly known as tunnel vision.

The week our final presentation was due, a friend of mine passed by with a distasteful look on her face as we were leaving school for the night. I need to let you know here, that the only time I'm on the receiving end of such an immobilizing glare is when I try to take the chew toy from my dog. This wasn't the case, so I needed to figure out what her problem was and fast. I pulled her aside and begged for some time alone with her. I prefaced the entire conversation with the hopes that she'd be as candid as possible with me. You always seem to regret it when you say something like that. Come to find out, I was the asshole in this situation without even knowing it.

This friend of mine was different from the rest of us. A little less outgoing, but when she finally did speak up, there was never any wasted air. She mentioned how the only thing I talked of throughout the semester was regarding the work I had been doing. She let me know that she felt I had forgotten to invest in the relationships of those around me. At first, like most cocky college students, I assumed this person was being all too sensitive and that they didn't have the work ethic I did.

After an extensive conversation and some time alone in my head, I came to the realization that I had become consumed in work and unknowingly lost sight of what mattered to me. I had such a thirst for a victory that I put my friends and family on the back burner. This exchange was sadly not the first time, nor the last, that I had been made aware of my unconscious actions; it was just the first time I acknowledged that I had to reorganize how I balanced my life.

Once I graduated, I went through peaks and troughs where I needed to deliberately remind myself of why I was working so hard and WHO had supported me for so long.

Being hard working is not an admirable trait if you forget why you're doing it in the first place.

Why? Because working hard without purpose is like exercising without the surge of endorphins causing that great feeling. We are putting in the effort and not experiencing any of the other benefits of living a balanced life! Now I look in the mirror in the mornings and can recall what and who motivates me to work so fervently. It also allows me to remember those I no longer communicate with because of my actions. At a young age, I realized how crucial keeping your personal life alive is key to your well-being and happiness.

Mental Health America exclaims that stress (or in this case a lack of balance) can weaken our immune systems and make us susceptible to a variety of ailments from common colds to something as severe as heart disease. The newest research shows that chronic stress can even double your risk of having a heart attack. That statistic alone is enough to raise your blood pressure!

While we all need a certain amount of stress to help us perform at our best, the key to managing stress and happiness lies in the word that I wasn't familiar with…balance. Not only is achieving a healthy work/life balance an attainable goal but workers, businesses, and people living their daily lives see the rewards. When workers, and people in general, are balanced and happy, they are more productive, take fewer sick days, and are more likely to stay in their jobs. Mental health studies continue to provide evidence that living to WORK and forgetting about balancing your life with free time, investing in relationships, and other things outside of work is just not healthy and, frankly, miserable.

Signs of the horrid tunnel vision are experiences like the one I went through. Have you noticed a different attitude from those you were once close to? Can you feel like all you've done is work and not spent any quality time with the people that mean the most to you? Do you even recognize the notion of "free time"? If you're connecting with the statements above, then you're on the same path I was, and it's an easy fix. You need to understand you've got some serious tunnel vision, confront it, and pay more attention in the future. Yes, it's going to be a consistent check in to make sure you're trying to balance, but I promise it is really easy.

"Unplugging" when I get home, focusing on things I love (motorcycle rides are like therapy sessions to me), and being in tune to how I feel helps me stay committed to a healthy work-life balance. By making these simple changes after my friend made it so apparent to me that I was losing control of my balance, I didn't become one of Employee Assistance Professionals Association statistics, which states that the number of stress-related disability claims by American employees has doubled! The EAPA also added that persistent stress can result in cardiovascular disease, sexual health problems, a weaker immune system, and frequent headaches, stiff muscles, or a backache. It can also lead to poor coping skills, irritability, jumpiness, insecurity, exhaustion, and difficulty concentrating. All this from just forgetting to take off the blinders (your tunnel vision) and reintroducing balance to such work focused life.

SO WHAT DOES THIS MEAN TO YOU?

Shawn Achor, a psychologist, touches on how happiness in our daily actions can impact our life. In The Happiness Advantage, Achor states that keeping our brains in "positive" mode versus negative, neutral, or stressed actually give us an enormous advantage in life and labour. He stresses how easy it is to influence our minds to embrace more happiness through our daily actions. I'm bringing that up because this simple change in my life has brought more happiness to my day-to-day. I make a conscious effort to balance my life with work, play, and the most important relationships in my life.

By just making time for these and taking the time for what's important to me, makes me happier in my work environment. I stay up later, wake up earlier, and I'm much happier doing it all because I do it all with balance.

You will always have deadlines and work that can easily fill your planner! There will always be daily frustrations and someone that tends to get in your way. Yet when you look at the lingering to-do list, do you have an answer as to why you fill your day and work so hard? Get your head away from you phone screen and look up!

There are people around you, friends supporting you, and family that adore you. You might not have all of that mentioned, but I will bet you have someone looking out for you. Make sure you never lose sight of them!

Never become so consumed by your work that you get lost in it and forget what motivated you to work so passionately in the first place! Remember to focus on the finish line, but never become so consumed by the marathon that you forget who or what is cheering for you on the sidelines! You can be passionate about what you do on a daily basis without becoming isolated! Put down this book and break out of the tunnel vision!

DAY 2 Completed: ____/____/_____

Write down those that have supported you no matter what. Can you say you've done the same?

Have you reminded them that they are appreciated? If not what is your reason?

What are you going to do today to make sure you don't get too consumed to remember those important to you?

How can you ensure you always remember this?

What did this mean to you?

"Because when you stop and look around, this life is pretty amazing."

—Dr. Seuss

DAY 3

- BE AN EXCEPTIONAL
COMMUNICATOR -

I left my bachelor pad bright and early (for a college senior that's 7:00 a.m.) in an excessively blissful mood. Not because it was a Friday morning or because it was my last semester of college, but because of the caffeine I treated myself to every Friday. As a creature of habit, I had fallen into a Friday routine, which just happened to involve stopping at my local gas station to grab a hot cup of coffee. I know it's gas station coffee, but if you didn't know any better would you care either? I didn't think so.

This was my last year of college, and somehow I avoided the addictive beverage, but the intensive marketing program I was part of quickly changed that. I was still dousing my coffee in cream and sugar and choked it down for the caffeine content. Due to the lack of coffee knowledge, I didn't care if I got a cup at Starbucks or at a gas station on the way to school, so as a college student with little income I had to choose convenience and value over anything else. This beer-budget lead me to the a.m./p.m. gas station on Alafaya, which was on the way to the college campus.

The employees were always sociable, but one in particular chose to go out of his way to make conversation. After visiting the same station and getting the same coffee, I began to build a relationship with the guy who rang up my coffee. This man, Gary, was working just to fund his dream of writing his own music and creating his own label. On this particular Friday, we talked a little while longer than normal, and I realized I was way behind schedule. Being late to a Professional Selling class is like being late for your wedding; you just don't do it, unless you're planning on filing divorce paperwork the same day you get married.

I sped off to class not to return to the gas station for over a month due to an unusually erratic schedule. After life had calmed down a little and summer was getting closer, I returned to the overly-happy Gary for my cup of crack. I made sure to ask about his musical endeavors and what he said shocked me.

A simple, but eye opening, "you remembered?!"

Let me remind you here, I do not have the best memory as most of my previous girlfriends can attest. I do not find myself listening all of the times I should be, thanks to growing up in a Greek family that happens to be firm believers in yelling over one another instead of listening. The mere fact that Gary was so surprised by me remembering should be an eye opener for anyone reading. The fact that I truly listened and did not just hear what Gary was saying allowed me to return and continue the conversation.

A lot of the time small talk is all that happens in interactions like this, and a lot of the same questions are asked because we weren't listening in the first place. Listening and remembering something that isn't directly impacting us is something we just don't do. Think about it. When someone brings up something you love, all of sudden you're all ears! You won't miss a piece of the conversation and can repeat the whole thing the next time you interact with the person. The same cannot be said for something you're not too keen on. For me, listening to Gary was something I could do in this instance because I was interested in the entrepreneurial spirit and music, so I listened. That's why it seemed so simple this time around.

It's been five years since that interaction, and I can say that taking the time to listen can help with more than just holding a conversation at the gas station register. With the time that has passed, it has allowed me to open my ears to things that I'm not necessarily interested in both my professional and personal life. It has allowed me to learn things that I might have missed (because I had my mind shut off), and it has helped me in multiple sales calls where I could find a solution to what truly is the source of a client's objection.

I have had failed relationships with significant others because I DIDN'T listen to what they wanted. Some of the best times I've had in relationships have been when I was listening and took a sincere interest in what was going on in the conversation. Why? Because I was present in the moment and the conversation. So whether it was positive, an argument, or something in between, I could contribute and, just like sales, provide insight or an apology. It's hard to say sorry if you don't know why and even harder to give insight if you don't know what you're giving advice on.

Listening is not something that should be an exception, but a rule of staying truly connected with what is going on! I mean when you have 35 SEPARATE business studies indicating listening is a top skill to be successful in business and life, do you really want to be the one person who doesn't put emphasis on being an exceptional communicator?

SO WHAT DOES THIS MEAN TO YOU?

Whether it is in your career or just everyday life, you will always have an opportunity to listen. I'm sure you've struggled trying to remember something and just can't pick it out in your busy mind. Some call that a brain fart. That's not a case of brain flatulence; that's you not LISTENING! You can't remember if you didn't listen!

Remember to take that opportunity every chance you get and you will be surprised at what is going on around you. Try not think about what you are going to say next, what text message just came across your phone, or if you just got a match on Tinder.

Listen to what the other person in front of you is saying or trying to say and you'll be able to contribute to the conversation and, ultimately, their day!

Sometimes participating is only listening and asking questions too. Have you ever talked someone's ear off and walked away saying how much you liked that person? You could have only learned that person's name and nothing else, yet you "like" them. Why? Because the greatest gift you can give anyone is listening and respecting what he or she has to say. Who doesn't love a gift?!

The challenge here is to LISTEN. Today stand out and be one of the exceptional communicators: an expert listener.

DAY 3 Completed: ____/____/_____

Write down ways you can make sure you listen today.

How do you think your day will be impacted by this?

Do you think you can tell the difference between the conversations and interactions you were really paying attention to and those you weren't?

What are you going to do to make sure you continue to take every opportunity to listen in the future?

What did this mean to you?

> *"To listen well is as powerful a means of communication and influence as to talk well"*
>
> *- John Marshall*

DAY 4

- LIVE FEARLESSLY -

I used to be someone who avoided risk at all cost. Even if I had to make up an excuse, I wasn't going to place my fragile body in harm's way. I was the child who didn't break a bone until I was living on my own in a college dormitory. It was more than just physical harm too. I avoided confrontation and any chance of rejection. I was like most human beings. Like psychologist Vivian Manning-Schaffel states, excuses to avoid confrontation stem from a fear of loss, pain, strain, or, this case, failure. It's seldom easy or enjoyable, and an easy way out is just simply to avoid it. That was all before popping my risk-adverse cherry.

In 2011, I chose to take some risks and never looked back.

I was moving from Central Florida to Savannah, Georgia, where I found myself working straight out of college for the medical company I was recruited by. Although I was going to be a short four hours away from everything I knew and loved, it was still a life-changing move. It was unsettling to realize that I would be leaving my family, friends, and all I had known for 21 years for this unknown risk.

I knew no one in Georgia, and the position I was accepting was a training position. I was about to jump into the deep end of a pool with no floaties on. If I learned how to swim on my own, the company would give me my own territory. If I failed, I'd be going back home with nothing to show for the risk I took. There was no promise of income or that'd I'd succeed. Fortunately, I survived and learned how to swim.

I was at the point where I had turned down opportunities because I was afraid, because I wanted to avoid rejection, or I just didn't "feel" like it. This opportunity to move to Georgia was the breaking point. Would I continue to live in this bubble or step outside of my comfort zone and live fearlessly on a more regular basis? I chose the latter. By taking the first step of just accepting the position I had already jumped into the unknown and was already fearlessly attacking an unfamiliar scenario. By assessing the risk versus the reward and understanding my short term goals (both of which we'll talk about later), I decided it was worth the chance. Those were some of the most rewarding moments in my life because I began to look at risk and opportunity differently. It allowed me to understand that fear was just something I created in my mind. It's something that just slows us down, and it is just a figment of our imagination.

Since that move, I have changed the way I look at my day-to-day. I accepted promotions that took me into uncharted territories for the company that had failed multiple times over for the opportunity of reward. I have said "yes" to things that would require some people to take a Xanax.* I've searched for an adrenaline rush in places I'd never thought I'd go.

---

* For those of you fortunate enough to have avoided this lovely drug, it's a drug used to treat anxiety and panic disorders. Think the modern innovation of breathing into a brown paper bag in drug form.

I'm not entirely crazy; I just realized that there was a lot more to live for if I just fought that paralyzing feeling of fear. The majority of concerns I had, were just made up in my mind anyway! Do I still fear things? Yes. What this taught me was to look at fear differently. Like I said, fear is in our imagination. We take the worst possible outcomes in the future and use it as a roadblock to STOP us from moving forward. Instead, remind yourself, as I do now, that fear is being pieced together by your imagination and creating a future that hasn't (and most likely won't) happen. USE that to live fearlessly.

SO WHAT DOES THIS MEAN TO YOU?

Plenty of people take risks much greater than the one I mentioned above. Keep in mind it is all relative to each individual! Think of a time when you were young, vulnerable, and had no income. Would you be content with leaving everything you knew behind to move somewhere with no friends or family? Some will say yes without a second thought. Others probably just had an anxiety attack and grabbed the paper bag next to their nightstand.

The point is, everyone is at different comfort levels when it comes to taking a risk. For example, Felix Baumgartner (an Australian skydiver, daredevil, and BASE jumper) is now known for skydiving to Earth from a helium balloon and falling over 24 miles. Do you think Felix woke up one morning and just decided to jump from space on his first free jump? No. He expanded his comfort zone

one jump at a time starting with his first world record parachute jump from a building in 1999. Then he moved on to being the first person to skydive across the English channel with a specially made carbon fiber wing in 2003. Step-by-step he expanded what "living fearlessly" meant for him.

You don't have to start by jumping off a building to begin living fearlessly. Pick something that scares the crap out of you and do it. You'll quickly find a lot of that fear is not real. There is always a chance of failure, but if you never take that risk and do that one thing that scares you, how would you know what would've happened? I'll help with that: you won't. The thought will hide in the back of your mind, and you'll just have that horrible "what if" feeling lurking like the weird uncle at Thanksgiving.

It doesn't matter if it is meeting someone new or skydiving; take the risk and reap the reward. It will either be a massive win for you or a learning experience, never a loss. Put your grown up pants on, take action, and do something that scares you today!

DAY 4 Completed: ____/____/_____

What are some things that scare you and you're avoiding because of it?

Is it dangerous or are you creating the "fear" in your mind?

If you ended up doing the things you were afraid of, how do you think you would feel?

Which calculated risk is one you're going to begin planning today?

How will you make sure you continue to take calculated risks?

What did this mean to you?

"Do one thing every day that scares you"

- Eleanor Roosevelt

DAY 5

- THERE IS NO "I" IN TEAM…
REALLY THOUGH -

One of the most invigorating experiences I've had the opportunity to enjoy in college was being part of the National Collegiate Sales Competition. Known as NCSC, top sales students from all over the nation role-played sales scenarios and were scored. It was the Olympics of the collegiate sales world with a National Sales Title for your school as the gold medal. It's the type of role-playing you use before a sales meeting, interview, or other objection based scenario. In life we role-play a lot of things—it's a way to engage our senses and experience something different. It's all practice for the real thing.

In this competition, there were "boxes" you needed to mark off as you sold your product to the randomly selected buyer on the other side of the table. Since the criterion was released ahead of the competition to prepare, teams were chosen months in advance. It was like preparing for a blind date with all the points you knew your partner would ask.

The teams of seven students were some of the most intense and competitive kids in the program. Quick-wits and sharp tongues made up the majority of the students selling in the competition. Many spent hours practicing during the months before and each teammate had a particular role. Our team went as far to have try-outs for the two select students on the team that would compete while the rest provided support.

By January 2011, first round try-outs were over, and we had our team of seven. After we had been selected, our professor explained we would have try-outs again. This time, it was for the two (competitor positions) spots of the competitor. The competitors were the ones going on the "blind dates" while everyone else prepped the questions. There was tension and contest amongst the team until the two competitors were chosen. I was one of those chosen to represent our program and university.

The anxiety among the group dissolved as we buckled down and turned all efforts towards the common goal of representing our college, our program, and our TEAM! We spent weekends, late nights, and any free time we could find reviewing scenarios, practicing possible objections, and prepping for every type of curve ball that could be thrown at us. I would be walking around on campus and a teammate would sit me down and start running through a role play scenario just to try to catch me out of my element. We were practicing like we were going to be playing in this competition.

The competition came and after the weekend, we walked away with third overall in the entire nation. Although it was devastating to see a third place instead of first, it was the journey that changed the way I would look at my future teams. It changed the way I'd look at my future teams because we sacrificed so much of our free time for a competition that wouldn't mean anything when we graduated other than memories. We believed in each other so ardently and devoted ourselves to the UNIFIED cause. We were all on the same page, with different strengths and roles and pushed towards the same cause. It showed me that a unified team was stronger than any one person. There is no way a single individual could compete and place on their own in that competition.

After experiencing this dangerous adult world, I realized how often we interact with teams throughout our lives. We work with teams on projects in employment that can determine how you get paid every quarter. We play in sports that all require teamwork and a team attitude. Even our relationships can be viewed a team dynamic! If you're not on the same page with your significant other, arguments frequently ensue. I am pretty familiar with that situation. Looking back at my teams, if there was a disconnect or lack of trust in one another, there was almost always failure. If everyone didn't understand their value, there was an even greater chance of failure. When there was devotion to one another and dedication to the collective goal, we surpassed expectations.

What this experience did for me was change the way I evaluated a successful team. Like Michael Jordan states, "Talent wins games, but teamwork and intelligence win championships." I realized that you can be the smartest person in the room, but if there is a task at hand that requires multiple skills and individuals, working alone can be detrimental. It taught me to quickly evaluate where people would be useful at in the team and if I didn't find out, I'd ask! It allowed me to quickly place roles (and value) on each team member. I found that when everyone had an understanding of the goal and knew the value they brought to the team, we were nearly unstoppable.

SO WHAT DOES THIS MEAN TO YOU?

Life will always hand you teams ranging from the organized teams of great skill to the scattered groups of seemingly weak links. Now take a moment to think about the most successful teams and think of the ones that have failed under pressure. The ones that move as one unit in sports or the sales team that works together are the ones that rise together.

The whole idea is to work with your team to complete a common goal to the best of your ability. The easiest way to accomplish that and survive the project with a positive experience is to believe in and support your team. Having someone believe in YOU can be incredibly empowering…imagine what would happen if everyone on the team felt the same way and everyone knew their role on the team!

If you ever find yourself straying away from the team orientation or you're part of a failing team, just remember there is no "I" in team. That also means that the team leader is not the only one holding everyone accountable. EVERYONE takes responsibility on the team. Make sure everyone on the team understands their roles, their value to the organization, and the common goal. This should also be pretty easy to remember because you really can't spell team with an "I." If you do, Google "Hooked on Phonics."

Today take the time to evaluate any teams you are on and make sure everyone is fighting for the same thing!

DAY 5 Completed: ____/____/_____

Write down a time you've been part of a failing team. Why do you think that was?

What about a time you've been part of a successful team? How and why was it different?

How can you make sure you always replicate the "successful" team mentality and use this today?

How are you going to approach team situations in the future to ensure stability and a true team orientation?

What did this mean to you?

"A Successful Team is a group of many hands and one mind"

– Bill Bethel

DAY 6

- THE FALL OF FINANCIAL LITERACY -

I grew up in a middle-class family with a roof over my head and food always on the table. From the time I was born to about high school, it was all sunshine and rainbows. It wasn't until my first job that I started to understand what earning a dollar meant and what my parents had done for years to keep us afloat. They worked so hard and were just promised an average retirement. In America, "normal" retirement means the children come back and help the parents because their 401(k) ran out. It doesn't sound like the "American dream" everyone is promised, right?

I'm not a parent yet, but I can value that as a parent you will do anything to make sure your children grow up better than you did. My parents did just that! I had been on vacations no child had the opportunity to go on and still remember the birthday parties my parents would host. Of course, all those things came at a cost, and to provide a wonderful childhood, a lot of those experiences were paid for with credit cards. My childhood cost my parents debt, and when I was old enough to understand this concept, I realized something our padded education system skips: there was a lack of financial literacy for the majority of Americans.

The difference between the guy down the street in the Ferrari and my parents was more than just a job or the badass car. It was the financial literacy one had versus the other. The financial experience that is passed down from parent to child and not taught in school. We'd much rather spend time on an SAT prep course than understand how to do taxes. Sadly, this is why only around 5% of people ever ascend or descend the economic class they grow up in. I could've easily accepted the traditional retirement plan, continued with the nine to five rat race, and retired at the ripe age of 70 with a 401(k). The thought of finally retiring and getting my diapers changed in a nursing home wasn't the "American dream" I was hoping for, so I'm taking the steps to make sure that didn't become reality.

My father did the same thing! He was born and raised with nothing. He had to buy his contact lenses in middle school because his parents couldn't afford them. Almost in poverty, he fought up the ladder to provide for his family. He had to educate himself on how to do that. By doing so, he provided a much more enjoyable childhood for my brother and me. As soon as I was old enough to understand what he went through, I promised I would do the same thing for my children and for my adult life. While growing up, I watched others that were successful and inquired as much as possible so that when I was ready I'd be prepared to start blazing my financial trail.

Immediately after I graduated, I went to a financial advisor and had a serious conversation. I explained my history and my lack of investment knowledge. I still remember telling him that I didn't have a dollar to my name and that if he gave me some financial direction that I would do business with him when I made some money. He agreed, and this kick-started my understanding of taxes, stocks, and the not-so-secret-secrets that a lot of people never find. I also spent plenty of time in books reading and learning as much as possible about money and how you can make it work for you! This was just the start of my actual education and how I'd make sure my children and their children would always be financially literate.

Think about it this way…if you never learned to drive what would you miss out on? Would you have been able to go to the beach over the weekend with all of your friends? Would you have been able to go to your prom with your date if you didn't have your driver's license? By not taking a simple driver's test and committing some of your time to learning how to drive, you miss out on so many opportunities. Financial literacy is the same. You can go and Google "the ten best ways to invest x-amount of money" right now. You could go and talk to a financial advisor tomorrow and explain, exactly as I did, that you have no idea what you're doing with your money. What happens if you don't?

Jere R. Behrman from the University of Pennsylvania thoroughly discusses how financial literacy affects wealth accumulation in his peer-reviewed study. He states that financial literacy and schooling attainment are both strongly positively associated with wealth outcomes. The data shows that they also indicate that the schooling effect only becomes active when combined with financial literacy. Plenty of people go to college but don't take the extra steps to understand what are the other ways you can make your hard earned cash work for you! As mentioned in the study, it can severely impact your long-term wealth accumulation.

SO WHAT DOES THIS MEAN TO YOU?

The rich stay rich and the poor get poorer. I hate that saying because it is only true if one does not do anything to change it. One of the most powerful things the rich have over the lower and middle-class is the financial literacy that isn't taught in our very broken school system. We go to college to earn a piece of paper with a school seal, some great memories, and improve our social awareness. We'll walk away with a job, a paycheck, and maybe a significant other, but don't understand how to itemize deductions on our taxes and invest in something other than a 401(k).

What this story really means is that you can find a number of resources to understand what you can do with your paycheck to ultimately make your money work for you. You alone have the power to change what your life will look like financially, how your children will live, and even how their children will live. We spend our college careers learning how to play the Olympic sport of beer pong, but never understand that we can write off certain expenses ever year to save on taxes. I'm sure being the MVP at the fraternity house party was a serious resume builder, but it's time to grow up.

Spend the time to learn what the rich have taught generation after generation, and you'll quickly find that the less fortunate only stay poor if they do not do anything about it! If you only know about a 401(k) or don't have a savings account, go out today and find out why. If you have both of those great! Go find out what the next financial milestone can be to you.

DAY 6 Completed: ____/____/_____

Where do you think you can improve your financial literacy?

What are you going to do about improving your financial literacy today?

How will you make sure you will always be improving your financial literacy?

What did this mean to you?

"It's not what happens to you, but how you react to it that matters"

- Epictetus

DAY 7

- THE 9 TO 5 MILLIONAIRE -

We live in a world of entrepreneurs and technology-literate people. Most of us were taught that if you wanted to escape the rat race, which our nation's workforce had fueled for so long, then you needed to start your own company or win the lottery. If you look at the statistics, you've got a greater chance of getting struck by lightning than winning the lottery. I don't know about you but I don't want to leave my life up to guesswork.

A 401(k) alone won't secure the "American dream" where you can vacation and experience all the things you couldn't at a young age. Baby boomers were coming to this conclusion faster than they wanted to, yet they still taught their children the way of the old "American dream." A study done by the Insured Retirement Institute stated that approximately four out of ten baby boomers have nothing saved for retirement. Then for those that have followed the "American dream" and saved, based off a report from BlackRock (Financial Planning & Investing), the average portfolio has only $136,200 in it. That leaves a retiree with $9,129.00 a YEAR to live off of for retirement. Sounds like poverty to me. I too was raised this way and believed in the original "American dream," until I was shown otherwise.

Due to the day-to-day grind that a sales job was known for, I had a hard time keeping up with current events. I like to know what is going on in the world outside of my personal bubble, so I chose to make CNN my homepage on my Internet browser. Facebook does an excellent job of updating me on some events, but you have to rummage through a lot of "this is why you're single" articles, and I don't need to be reminded of that. This allowed me to stay updated on current events and enjoy the occasional feel-good story on the front page.

One morning, a headline caught my eye that didn't have to do with war or another shooting.

CNN had interviewed a 27-year-old millionaire. This wasn't typical for our generation, but this story was unique. This young man had accumulated a net worth of $1 million through the stock market, key investments in an IRA, and real estate. He didn't have liquid assets of $1 million, but his total net worth was over $1 million. It might seem like a lot in today's world, but keep in mind most Americans don't even have a savings account.

So what was his secret? He spent the time learning about the different ways to make his money work for him discussed in the last chapter. By finding different ways to invest and doing his own research he became a nine to five millionaire and won't have to rely on his 401(k) to retire. He also won't be retiring at the old age of 70 years old.

This young gun worked an ordinary job. He didn't start his own company or win the lottery. He found ways to work towards his goal of financial freedom and found it through different investment vehicles.

So who cares what this random 27-year-old did? You should because this could be you. This story, along with so many others, proves that millionaire status is not reserved for the professional athletes, entrepreneurs, and movie stars. A New York Times study further dispels the common myths about the millionaire next door, by stating the average millionaire total household income (taxable) is $131,000, and they live on less than 7% of their wealth! This is all just extra data showing that it's not ever too late to reach the nine to five millionaire status. Stop thinking outside the box and forget about the box altogether. There is one person in charge of achieving that nine to five millionaire status…it's you.

SO WHAT DOES THIS MEAN TO YOU?

So many people take the lazy route of a mere 401(k) and hoping the 401(k) will be there at 65. Their savings account is empty just waiting for the financial windfall from the lottery. Unfortunately, you have a lower chance of winning the lottery than that sweet pickup line you just used working. History has also shown that a 401(k) will not be able to support most lifestyles alone and can't even be used until 65. Will you know how your body is going to be working at 65? Neither do I, but I highly doubt my liver will be in any good working order. So why wait to set up a life for 65 that might not even come to fruition?

At first glance, the only way to change this is by starting your own venture or winning the lottery. If you've got a great idea, go for it! If you win the lottery, congrats, I'll send you my mailing address.

So what about you and me? The "normal" people.

Luckily, there are more options than accepting your fate in the working-class rat race. Take what we talked about in the last chapter and use this story as motivation. Anyone can be a millionaire by his or her own means and you don't have to buy a lotto ticket or create the next Facebook. With some extra research and by finding other ways to make your income work for you, the nine to five millionaire status becomes attainable. How are you going to do it? If you can't answer that, you need to put this down and start figuring it out or find someone who has the result you are looking for and ask for help, insight, and the resources you need. This is your future, so you're going to need to put some effort and work into how it turns out.

DAY 7 Completed: ____/____/_____

What are some different ways you can reach your nine to five millionaire status?

Which one of those can you put into play today? How?

Did something from the increase in your financial literacy help with this?

How are you going to make sure you continue marking off ways to reach your nine to five millionaire status?

What did this mean to you?

"The bad news is time flies — the good news is you're the pilot"
— Michael Altshuler

DAY 8

- DO SOMETHING NICE WITHOUT GETTING CAUGHT -

Anytime there was alcohol involved in my young adult life, it seemed like the following morning always started with Advil and water with a splash of Pedialyte*. It was the breakfast of champions for me in my early 20s. I've since upgraded to multi-vitamins and proper breakfast foods to start the day. Of course, before the latter mentioned, I had my fair share of "forgotten" nights. The one I'm about to share was one that reinforced my hope in humanity: there are good people out there.

---

* Pedialyte is designed to prevent dehydration and replace lost electrolytes for infants and adults.

The 5:00 a.m. sun had crept into the staircase of my new apartment building and reminded me I was hung-over. I glanced around and realized I was on the staircase of my new apartment in Savannah, Georgia. I tried to remember how I got there, but all I could think of was how badly my head hurt. I had recently moved to Savannah from Sanford, Florida to start my new career out of college, and I was lucky enough to find a new group of friends rather quickly. I had the help from Chad, my co-worker, who was more outgoing and suave than most sales people I had met. He had a way with people that someone can only be born with. About three months into the job, I was invited to a themed wedding held on the rooftop of one of the buildings down by the waterfront.

Like many, I celebrated a little too much and, unfortunately, ended up with no memory of anything between the hours of midnight to 5:00 a.m. That's five hours of my life that disappeared. Whoever creates a black box (like a flight recorder) for daily living will be a very successful person! Normally, the hangover is the worst part for an irresponsible 21-year-old, but not for this guy. Life was my teacher, and I was the kid who just got put in the corner for a time out.

Around 10:00 a.m. that morning, my friendly neighbor across the hall began knocking on my door. She was a chipper, brunette that loved to share the experiences she had in her daily life. The stories were always hilarious, so I always entertained them, but I just wasn't in the mood that morning. Reluctantly, I opened my door, and she gladly handed me the coat to my suit. Apparently, I had waltzed up the stairs the night before stripping down to cool off leaving my suit pieces along the different levels of the apartment. I was a next level Chip 'n' Dale without the washboard abs. I did the quick once over of my suit and my pockets only to realize my wallet was gone.

I immediately began searching for my wallet, retracing my steps from the night before. I called my new group of friends, and they couldn't recall where I was for almost three hours. It was hopeless. I tried to delay canceling my credit cards as long as possible, but by the next morning, I realized it was time to move on and accept that I wasn't going to find it. My Florida driver license, which was a crucial part of my career as a driving sales rep, was also included in the assortment of plastic I had lost. This made driving across southern Georgia and trying to purchase things with just a credit card number extremely challenging. An "IOU" at a restaurant doesn't ever work out.

This all happened on Sunday morning, so by Thursday of that week, I had received most of my cards back, including my ID from Florida's Department of Transportation.

Along with all the new cards, what I didn't expect was a phone call from my mother explaining she had a received a package with my wallet in it. I was excited to have my wallet back, even though I already had replaced everything in it. It was more piece of mind knowing someone didn't go on a shopping spree. What was fun was trying to explain exactly how my wallet ended up being mailed to my mom. She was never too excited about how I spent my nights out, but this one pissed her off.

Along with my wallet came a handwritten note. A man had found my wallet, requested that I not send a reward, and only wrote: "I'd hope you'd do the same for someone else." He simply found my ID and sent the package to the address, which was my parent's home since I had just graduated. This meant that this guy had held on to my wallet all night and then spent the next day driving to a post office to get it back to its rightful owner.

This experience taught me that paying it forward was much more than making sure everyone knew you were doing it. It taught me that paying forward is more about doing what is right in your mind with or without the recognition. Now for me, if I come across an opportunity to do something like this, I just think of myself in the other person's shoes. Would I want them to do "x" for me? The majority of the time I can answer yes and end up going out of my way to pay it forward. The other fraction of the time I end up thinking about what I could have done and realize it wasn't going to take that much time to go a little out of my way to make someone's day.

Being on the receiving end of this, I realized that the minor portion of your day spent helping someone in need is trivial compared to the relief and joy you give the recipient. That man did not need to ship my wallet, write a letter, or even pick up my wallet for that matter. He honestly could have had some free drinks the rest of the night on me and left me to deal with the fraud complaints with the credit card company.

SO WHAT DOES THIS MEAN TO YOU?

Every day we have opportunities to do something that is out of our way or not worth our precious time. More often than not, we are too engulfed in our day.

We are in too much of a rush to realize the cashier is having a horrible day.

Too busy to realize the $20 bill just dropped from that girl's purse and way too busy to return it.

Next time you find one of those opportunities, don't be afraid to take a little extra time out of your "busy" schedule to help out. This might come as a shock to some, but the world doesn't revolve around a single person!

What would you want someone to do for you if you were in that same situation? Just because no one is watching you do something for someone else, doesn't mean it didn't happen. Keep your eyes and ears open today for an opportunity to make someone's day.

DAY 8 Completed: ____/____/_____

How many times a day do you think you miss an opportunity to help someone in need?

What will you do today to make sure you "make" someone's day?

How can you make sure you keep your mind open to opportunities to make a difference in the future?

What did this mean to you?

"The measure of a man's real character is what he would do if he knew he never would be found out"

- Thomas Babington Macaulay

DAY 9

- THANK YOU? -

No matter how small or how great the act of kindness, most parents bred us to say thank you. My mother was almost psychotic about it, getting somewhat upset if someone else didn't say thank you or lacked any manners in general. "Josh," she'd say after I received a new toy from someone, "What do you say?!". That's just the way I was brought up. Something she did a little differently, though, was the cards. The rare hand-written thank you card is still something that she does to this day.

Writing thank you cards became a weekly (sometimes daily) endeavor in the Professional Selling Program. I became so accustomed to writing thank you cards that I continued to do so after graduation for any prospective client that sat down and spent time with me. The amount of cards I have received back in the mail, either because I had the wrong address or the recipient also decided to say thanks, is overwhelming. I have even seen the thank you cards placed on the walls with our cards right next to them. It wasn't the fact that these sometimes brought new business or that the offices we worked with would put them on the wall; it was the way it made some of these people feel! I still remember my first "Return to Sender" card and how it affected the recipient

While in Savannah, I decided I was going to hand deliver a letter that had been returned to the sender. I made sure to drop into the office right before 5:00 p.m. to make sure I saw the person it was meant to go to. After giving the letter away, and explaining why it was covered with "Return to Sender" stickers, the office manager spent some time talking to me. She was appreciative of what my partner and I took the time to do. She also spent a moderate amount of time mocking how horrible my penmanship was. To be fair, my handwriting was similar to that of a person writing with a vibrating pencil. The office manager was saying how nice the card was when she mentioned that other accounts should be working with us. She reminded me that I needed to call on one of her family members at a large client in Tifton, Georgia.

My sales rep and I followed up with the lead Friday afternoon and found that the office manager had called to let the office know we were going to stop by. Not only that, but apparently our office manager had only good things to say about us. It was like having a friend introduce you to a girl or guy you like. You all of sudden have much more credibility than you would have if you approached them on your own.

We did nothing special with this office but sent them a few simple thank you cards, and in return, we received a personalized invitation to some new business.

This is something that we've gotten away from in the fast-paced world we are in today. So many people are tied to their phones and email and just forget to say a simple thank you. Personalizing a card takes more time, so for a generation used to instant gratification, this just isn't feasible. I think the digital world has taken the personality and personal touch out of a lot of thank you cards, birthday wishes, and condolences for a friend. These are all perfect examples that don't involve a sales call, where you can utilize the lost art of saying thank you (even on a folded piece of stationary).

It's much more than just two words as Martin Nowak, the director of Harvard's program for Evolutionary Dynamics, discusses in one of his studies. "Thanking is a form of cooperative reciprocity with roots in primate behavior." For Paula Madden, a real estate developer in Portland, Oregon, "Good manners are the basis of civilization." As illustrated above, thanking someone with more than just a text or email is so much more than a sweet sentiment.

SO WHAT DOES THIS MEAN TO YOU?

Thank-you cards are not meant to gain new business or get on anyone's good side, although they can. They are intended to show gratitude and sheer appreciation…period. If you are grateful for something, why not show it with a simple stamp and a quick *personalized* "thank you"? Fortunately, you can do this for anything and in any environment. It does not need to be exclusively for your business!

I also want to make sure you see *personalized* italicized. I emphasized that because personalizing anything adds an extra touch that show's you aren't just creating cookie cutter notes. The interaction, experience, or gift was unique, so why not spend a few extra seconds adding that personal touch? Once again it comes full circle…how would you feel after receiving a thank you card? Seeing something in the mail with your name on it is uplifting and feels like Christmas!

Why not share that pleasant feeling with those around you? Today, go home and think of someone you need to show some gratitude towards. It doesn't need to be a card, maybe just a phone call. Just remember to reach out and thank someone that needs it today.

DAY 9 Completed: ____/____/_____

What does it feel like to get a thank you card in the mail? What about any form of sincere gratitude?

What will you do this week to make sure you're showing gratitude and appreciation to the people who earn it?

What are you going to do to make sure you show appreciation in the future when someone deserves it?

What did this mean to you?

"The smallest act of kindness is worth more than the grandest intention"

– Oscar Wilde

DAY 10

- REJECTION WON'T KILL YOU -

The company I started with was so different from most pharmaceutical companies. Unlike a lot of pharmaceutical sales reps, we didn't just walk in for a signature and hope our service was prescribed. Our business revolved around asking doctors to use our service and not just sign a piece of paper. We had to show enough value to these doctors, so that they would consciously use our service in the middle of their day. When I first started, I worried far too much what other people thought, so I was a little careful with how much I asked for on a sales call. I was worried that the doctor might say no, the situation might get awkward, or worst of all they might not like me anymore.

Four months into my career, the rep I was working with, Chad, gave me two choices for a lunch appointment I was about to go into. He was sending me to the meeting alone with a simple goal. This is the same guy that could talk himself out of any situation, so the idea of a "simple" goal to me was all in the eye of the beholder.

He wanted me to ask for the business until the doctor said yes and signed up or kicked me out. When he said that, my blood pressure went up, and I broke into a sweat. It wasn't the balmy southern weather either; it was because I immediately realized that this meeting was going to get uncomfortable. I was reluctant to accept the challenge and almost had a panic attack before I walked in, but I now know why he told me to do it.

I pushed so hard for the business that the physician was yelling at me about how he disagreed with almost everything I said. To be fair, it's not too hard to get an arrogant doctor to yell at you if you sound as inexperienced as I did. I continued to take some verbal abuse until I selected a few buzzwords I'd heard Chad use. By the end of the conversation, he calmed down and did agree to a trial with us, which wasn't a full business deal but the next best thing.

The real learning experience here was that I walked out unscathed. The yelling, the "no," and all of the disagreement did not hurt me. If that was the worst thing that can happen in an office call, then I can handle anything!

There are so many articles and studies done on how rejection plays a serious part in our lives. It's almost as apparent as approval is in our lives. Dr. Carmen Harra, a best-selling author and clinical psychologist, wrote a piece for the Huffington Post stating, "Rejection, as an ego-reducing emotion, is nothing short of painful. But viewing rejection as necessary and even positive will help you overcome it that much more easily." Nowhere in the entire write-up did she say it would kill the person on the receiving end. There is a doctor here saying that the only thing rejection hurts is your ego. So what do we do now when we run into the ever-present "rejection"? Remember it's not going to kill you and take it as a learning experience!

SO WHAT DOES THIS MEAN TO YOU?

Five years after that experience, I still have Chad to thank for motivating me to step far outside of my comfort zone and get awkward. Taking that first step to get outside of my comfort zone was just the start too. Understanding that a "no" or disagreement physically cannot hurt you but can change the way you approach situations in your personal life and sales career.

You begin to ask questions you never would before because you do not mind if the response is yes, no, or something worse. You know that no matter what that verbal response is, it isn't going to kill you. If you see a guy or girl you really like and haven't talked to, how will you ever know what could've happened if you don't talk to them? What about the great business decision that could alter an industries landscape or increase your pay? How would you know what could have happened if you don't ask? Just go and ask for it.

I challenge you to ask one more question today. You might get a horribly uncomfortable response, but you're still going to walk away alive! Keep going until you get the answer you want! Today you will realize words don't kill you.

DAY 10 Completed: ____/____/_____

Write down things that could be different if you just ASKED for them today.

Which one of the above are you going to do this week? Write down how they turned out.

What are you going to do to remember that rejection won't hurt you and continue to ask for what you want in the future?

What did this mean to you?

"It's not about how hard you can get hit. It's about how hard you can get hit and keep moving forward."

- Rocky Balboa

DAY 11

- THE DAILY GOAL -

In the fast-paced world of sales, goal setting runs rampant. Goals on daily numbers were the most prevalent and also the most abused. After a while, setting "goals" starts to lose its effect on a sales force, especially if they don't know how to reach those goals. Fortunately, the company I was part of for so long had an excellent group of leaders that directed us on how to create realistic and attainable goals, which resulted in much more follow through.

Although some goals were based on personal development at our company, we also had our share of numbers-based goals. As with many sales forces in this world, numbers-based goals were tied to you (the salesperson) meeting or surpassing your quota (what you're expected to sell). Meeting or exceeding that quota meant a nice commission check at the end of the month. What you killed is what you ate at the end of the day in any sales job.

Those who reached our companies outrageous goals sometimes received unique rewards, such as a Rolex, and were even listed in President's Club for the year. President's Club is the highest honor you can get in a sales force. It normally includes a select group of sales professionals that exceeded their goals for the year and were subsequently awarded an exotic trip, time away from work, a cash bonus, or something else that could motivate them for the following year's goals. Remember when you were five, and you received a gold star for running the fastest mile? President's Club is like that is except you are much older and don't get to take a nap in the middle of the day.

The greatest feeling of accomplishment I had at my first sales job was when I made it into that group and got to enjoy a President's Club trip to Cabo San Lucas, Mexico. This was a big deal for me because the year before we missed our numbers to make President's Club by a minuscule amount. Although the growth numbers the year before were staggering, we still didn't reach our goal as a team, so I spent some time with my manager at the time, Kristen.

She spent so much time with our team in the Los Angeles territory and with the rest of her region. Kristen always reminded me of the goals we set AND how we were getting there, making sure every moment was a learning experience. She made sure we were choosing different strategies, different types of offices to call on, and that we had a different way of looking at reaching the goal we had set. She made sure that we didn't just look at the big picture but had a goal to reach every single day.

Just in this particular example, we were required to write down the numbers that we needed to work towards to reach President's Club. This was our big picture goal. Then with that set, each day we had a goal that pushed us towards that number. This included setting lunch meetings, making cold calls, and closing business each day. Then on top of that, we had monthly and quarterly "checkpoints" we had to make to ensure we were on track.

When we were able to earn a spot in President's Club, Kristen was there at the end of the stage still cheering us on. She was there at the end of the ceremony, knowing she had a direct impact on every single award recipient that year based on goal setting alone!

This is just an example used in my sales career, but this goal setting mentality can be used in our daily lives as well. I'm a little obsessive with writing my goals down and I think that's important. I've written down a lot of my personal long and short-term goals. Then I've set checkpoints both yearly, quarterly, and daily. An excellent example of this (which we'll go into detail later on) is the real estate I've acquired. It took three years from the idea to pulling the trigger, but I made it happen because I set daily goals of saving a specific amount of money and reading a specific amount of real estate text to prep for my first purchase. Goal setting in everyday life can be just as impactful as it is for a successful sales professional.

Why listen to just me? Let's check with the some of the most intelligent students in the nation. A study done with Harvard MBA students in 1979 showed that 84% of the MBA program had no particular goals, 13% had goals that weren't committed to paper, and only 3% had clear, written goals and plans to accomplish them. Skip to 1989, and the interviewers again checked in with the 1979 graduating class. The results were not too surprising. The 13% with goals were earning, on average, twice as much as the 84% with no goals at all. The 3% who had clear, written goals were earning, on average, ten times as much as the other 97% put together.

The only variable factor in this study was the way these students set their goals and put it into play. If that doesn't make you want to change the way you set your goals, I don't know what will.

SO WHAT DOES THIS MEAN TO YOU?

No one is a stranger to 'goals." Everyone creates goals that they strive for each and every day, but they don't have directions on how to get there! In regards to goals, I keep two things in mind now, which were all kick started by the above experience.

First, goals can be set that range from tomorrow to your last day. What are your personal and professional goals one year, five years, and ten years from where you're at now? Do you have a clear picture? Do you have any answer at all? If you don't or it still seems unclear, sit down today, tonight, or tomorrow, think about it, and WRITE it down. It's so important that you have some goal or picture of where you want to be in your future and have it on paper.

How frustrating is it to get home from grocery shopping and find that you forgot an essential ingredient to your dinner? If you just wrote it down, you would have remembered it. If I could cook something other than ramen, then I'd relate to that feeling as well, but I digress. If you can write down your grocery list, why wouldn't you do that for your life goals and dreams as well?

There is no time limit on how long it should take. The key here is making sure you set it and don't forget it. Set your goal and work backward making sure you have checkpoints and reminders along the way. It's a way of checking the pulse on your progress. Are you close?

Second, goals do not have to be as number oriented like the one in this story. As a sales professional, most of my career-oriented goals were correlated directly to my pay and numbers. Of course, I had plenty of personal goals that involved developing myself as an individual. For example, while in a leadership role, I would always wake up in the morning and dive for my phone. It just added to my anxiety and so I set steps to improve that, and within a year, I had no problem waking up and starting my day on my own time, instead of diving for my phone.

Remember to write down your personal and professional goals and write down the steps to get there. With constant reminders and checkpoints along the way, you'll not only feel more accomplished, but you will have a much higher chance of reaching that goal that seems so impossible! Do you have some hopes and objectives that you have yet to accomplish? Write them out today.

DAY 11 Completed: ____/____/_____

Write down where you want to be professionally next month, one year, five years, and ten years from now.

Write down where you want to be personally next month, one year, five years, and ten years from now.

What are going to do today to accomplish one of your personal and professional goals?

What is your plan to accomplish your professional and personal goals in the future?

What did this mean to you?

"Without goals, and a plan to reach them, you are like a ship that has set sail with no destination."

- Fitzhugh Dodson

DAY 12

- EXCUSE ME SIR, I'M DIFFERENT -

My alarm went off at 6:30 a.m. and I jumped out of bed. It was a typical Tuesday morning in Los Angeles, California with no humidity and a lot of sunshine. This was one of those mornings where everything seemed like it was going to exceed my expectations. I had just recently moved to Los Angeles for a promotion from Savannah. My partner and I finally had our territory tracking at record growth, and, as a result, my ego was through the ceiling. I didn't expect the new hire who was riding with me that day to hit me across the face with some needed humility.

Once you had hit a certain point in your career at this company and upper management felt like you had a good sense on what was going on, new hires were occasionally sent to you with hopes of picking up good habits. Most of the new hires that rode with me were fresh out of college or from an entirely different industry. Many had very little sales experience, which meant a ride along was spent teaching them about basic sales skills instead of our service. The new hire I had this particular day was different…

The new hire had recently accepted a job with us and was an ex-device rep. He spent time in the surgery rooms with doctors, selling them the metal pieces that went into a lot of patients. If you had a synthetic body part surgically put in, he most likely sold it to your doctor. He was great at what he did and was extremely personable. Throughout the day, I checked in with him on what we would review on each office call, how he was feeling, and if there was anything he'd do differently. Our last meeting of the day was at 4:00 p.m. in Ventura, which was a good hour west of Los Angeles. I remember being overly aggressive and making sure we walked out with a signed registration.

We got back to my car and began our long haul through traffic. I asked for the new hire's opinion on what he would have done differently and where I could improve. I was so confident at this point that asking was more out of formality than honestly looking for criticism. The new hire was quick to point out that I did an excellent job, but he felt I could have approached the physician in a different way to get a better response. The new hire noted the way I approached the doctor was similar to every other salesperson that had walked in there. Instead, he said to act as a resource, and instead of pushing a product or service, get on the side of the person you're selling to. Partner up with the person across the table instead of going to battle with them! Showing someone that you're different and that you are a resource can mean the difference between a big win in sales and a significant waste of time. I had heard this before, but it's different when you hear it from an outside perspective... I was acting like EVERY other sales rep..

Again, this an example of sales call and being a different salesperson compared to the next one. Let's bring it closer to home and relate it to EVERYONE. Have you been on a job interview before? Almost every single reader of this book has been through one, and for those who haven't, a job interview is a meeting with a potential employer designed solely to give the opportunity to STAND OUT from the rest of the candidates! Just like the sales call I struggled to show how I was different from all the other reps, an interview (and a lot of other interactions in life) is an opportunity to scream out how you're different!

For data and factual evidence on how important it is to stand out in job interviews, sales calls, and everyday life, turn to Google. Type in "why it is important to stand out" and you'll find studies from Harvard, business journals, and articles from some of the most successful people out there exclaiming how important it is to remind everyone that YOU'RE different!

SO WHAT DOES THIS MEAN TO YOU?

If you've read any book on personal development, you have read about "being different." If you have been in a sales career for any amount of time, you've been told to "differentiate" yourself. Hopefully it doesn't take an experience like mine to realize that all these books and coaches really speak the truth. Ask yourself, "How am I different from the other sales professionals that have walked in here?" Do you have an answer? If not, here is your opportunity to think it through and develop a response. If you can't differentiate yourself from the other guy in a suit and tie, you'll end up being another statistic.

This applies to more than the average sales professional as well! We are all unique in our own ways. Do you want to be just like that person sitting to the right of you? What about being identical to your significant other? No. You want to be different. If you can't think of a way that you differentiate yourself, professionally or personally, take tonight to think about it. How will you differentiate yourself in your next face-to-face conversation?

DAY 12 Completed: ____/____/_____

What do you think makes you different from the person next you?

How will you use your unique differences to stand out this week at work and in your personal life?

What do you plan on doing in the future to ensure you continue to differentiate yourself in your daily life?

What did this mean to you?

"In order to be irreplaceable, one must always be different"

- Coco Chanel

DAY 13

- IGNORE THE WHITE NOISE -

I had been the team lead for our territory for over a year, and we just added another team member. That meant I was leading a group of two people with no prior leadership experience. It was the blind leading the blind. With all of that going on, I started to notice a difference in my original partner that was going to impact the entire team. This wasn't going to be an easy conversation.

Originally there were just two of us. Myself and one other person tasked with growing a territory. We doubled business for two years in a row and made it to Presidents Club for the second year. During that second run at Presidents Club, one of my teammates began to show a lack of excitement and motivation. I had become so accustomed to their energy that I noticed an obvious drop-off. I did what I thought was the right thing…I brought up my observation and stated we needed to sit down and talk this out. I was that guy in the relationship that "just wanted to talk." They reluctantly agreed.

By the time we had scheduled our meeting, we were already four months into having a third teammate. Now, every action affected two people instead of just myself and one other. Instead of personalizing each encounter, I had to make the right choices for the unit as a whole. The talk ended with my coworker confessing that they wanted to leave the company and began searching for a job. They prefaced that portion of the conversation by questioning whether they could trust me not to mention this conversation.

My response was simple…if it didn't impact the entire team, then I would keep my mouth shut. Obviously, that wasn't the case, so I gave them the opportunity to tell upper management. If they didn't do it, I was going to have to do it. They were worried about bringing it up and, at first, was vehemently against the idea, but by the next week, they had taken it upon themselves to have the hard conversation with leadership. After this, the relationship we had outside of work was never the same, and for a long time after that conversation, I questioned if I did the right thing.

As someone with a decision like this to make, it's not about how you feel at the end. Like I said, I was still conflicted with my decision because I'm an emotional person. It's more about if you made the conscious effort to ignore the white noise or your emotional and personal attachment. By ignoring the personal and emotional attachment I had, I was able to focus more on what was right for the team and, in the end, make a decision that was the best for the team and not just one person! I learned that by ignoring all the white noise, I was able to focus on the most efficient and logical decision for the team as a whole.

SO WHAT DOES THIS MEAN TO YOU?

For most people in leadership roles, the daily grind is not the most stressful part of the job. Hard conversations, letting someone go, and making or delegating decisions are all (literally) part of the job description. It is the mental battle that happens when a leader must make a decision for the greater good of the TEAM over one person. No matter how many times you do it, you never get used to it. I had to look at this issue and realize I was making a decision for the entire team and keep the personal relationship out of the conversation.

Think about the personal attachment, relationship, and emotional involvement as white noise. It provides escalating distraction and impacts your true focus on a decision that is affecting more than just one person! You've got to be able to ignore the white noise and focus on the decision in a logical sense and ignore the other distractions.

It was the first time I had to do something like this and it was harder than turning down a pint of Ben and Jerry's (for those of you who know me, that's worse than physical torture). But one thing I realized is that not everyone is going to like you or agree with you, so why try to appease everyone? The next time (or your first time) you find yourself in a situation where one person's actions could affect an entire team, separate your personal feelings towards the person and think about the whole team. When you think of the whole team, you're thinking big picture and ultimately what the long term impacts are.

DAY 13 Completed: ____/____/_____

Have you had to make a decision where the result impacted more than one person? What happened?

If you think big picture more often than not, how would that change the way you made decisions today?

How are you going to make sure that you keep the big picture in mind when making decisions impacting more than one person in the future?

What did this mean to you?

"The man who wants to lead the orchestra must turn his back on the crowd"

- James Crook

DAY 14

- SUCCESS APATHY -

My second National Sales meeting for my career in sales had concluded at the beginning of 2012, and I was walking out with a difference of opinion. I had been with the company for just over eight months and earned my first promotion. The majority of training representatives (including myself) were going to be starting new roles as territory sales representatives. This just meant that we had a territory of our own! So what was I so divided on?

The Vice President closed us out with a speech and did an excellent job at inspiring all of us, as he normally did. One thing he would not let us forget was that he hated the word success. He reminded us that success breeds complacency. This can be true, but even he believed there were exceptions to that.

Spending time in a high-energy, fast-paced job like sales, can introduce you to both sides of success. I had the chance to see veteran sales representatives quadruple a territory one year and then completely throw in the towel. They would hit their numbers one time and just feel that they had reached the pinnacle of their "success." They looked at success as if it was permanent and that it lasted forever. They were sadly mistaken. These reps over the years burned out, quit, or were fired.

2014 was the year I realized a closed account or successful couple of months wouldn't last forever. We were on track to hit the goal, and I pressed cruise control. Our team missed it by 2%. The team I was part of had so many shout-outs during the year, and we had done so well. I called us successful and took my foot off the gas pedal for a short amount of time. I became complacent and missed the final mark for my team and me. Why? Because I fell into the routine I had become accustomed to and believed what I had done for the majority of the year was going to continue right through to the finish line. Instead of continuing to work like I had for the first half of the year, I expected the business I had grown to carry me to the finish line. I was wrong and paid for it. For those of you who don't realize it, in life, and especially sales, the past doesn't count; it's only today and tomorrow.

Why do you think there are underdog stories in sports? Because what I'm trying to explain here happens to the championship team. They get complacent thinking that all of the work they have done, all the practice they've had will carry them to the next championship. What happens is the fire they first had can be found in the "underdog" team. This isn't a question of persistence or focus. It's just the symptom of falling into a routine where we become all too comfortable.

Then there is the other side of success. The exception to the rule: the group that uses their past success as tinder for a much greater fire. They take past successes and use it as a fuel to reach the next goal or dream. There's the motivation, "heart," and passion I've been talking about this entire book.

The following year after missing presidents club by 2%, our team doubled the territory and blew by our goals by 20%. We did not take our foot off the gas pedal one time the entire year, even when it seemed like we had reached our goal early. We worked as hard as our bodies and minds could handle until we were walking across the stage to claim our award. Success did not breed complacency the second time around. The stage was our finish line for that year, and we were Olympic athletes.

How many times have you seen an Olympic athlete stop short of their goal? Only the ones that haven't made a spot on the podium stop short. The ones that win multiple times are the people who don't get comfortable in a routine and always keep their body and mind guessing. They know that if they become complacent and don't train as hard (or harder) as they did the year they won, they'll succumb to somebody who is. They know success can breed complacency, but these winning Olympic athletes only use it as fire!

SO WHAT DOES THIS MEAN TO YOU?

Success can breed complacency. I've seen it on a regular basis at work and our personal lives. Have you ever heard of a one-hit wonder? We all have—you know, the one hit wonders that believed they had reached the epitome of "success" and put their life into cruise control. What happened to those people? They fade away. Think about the singles on iTunes you never hear again.

Now think of someone you know that, in your mind, has been successful and continues to do so. Have they stopped what made them successful in the first place? Not even a little. These people don't ever let off the gas even though they blast through any challenge that comes their way.

Although I tend to avoid television and watching sports, athletes are an excellent example of this.

Select athletes, like Michael Jordan, are known for multiple championships and MVP awards. He didn't stop practicing at his first championship. He didn't cease to be successful, even after he was done playing basketball!

You choose what kind of impact the extraordinary word "success" has on your life. Make sure each success in your life is just a stepping-stone to your next destination in your journey, not a place to settle down.

DAY 14 Completed: ____/____/_____

When have you used success as a motivational fire? What happened?

Write down some successes that you've used as stepping stones to your next grand success?

What can you do today to use a past success to motivate you?

How will you make sure you continue to use your success as a fuel and not a hindrance in your future?

What did this mean to you?

> *"The biggest mistake to me is complacency"*
>
> – Bonnie Hammer

DAY 15

- ACTION SPEAKS LOUDER THAN WORDS -

The owner of the company I had dedicated three years of my professional career to was about to make an appearance for the first time since 2011. During the exponential growth of the company he took a leave of absence and to continue the upward trend, he passed the reigns over to our upper management team and had faith in the sales force. The growth did not fade while he was gone, and in 2014, the owner and founder decided it was a good time to remind the sales force where the company had come from.

Our owner, like most entrepreneurs, realized there was a problem. There was an issue with the way pain management patients were cared for, and he had first-hand experience. Not only that, but he could solve the problem and change a stagnant industry. After seeing the opportunity and finding the answer to how his company would sustain and grow, he acted. The following months were spent sleeping on couches and spending every cent he had on the creation of his dream. Keep in mind, all this happened before Kickstarter and other crowdfunding platforms, meaning he had to find all this funding himself.

Now in front of his sales force, the owner finished the story with the explanation of just how in awe he was. Not because the majority of the sales force was in their 20s, but the fact that in a few short years we had become a billion-dollar company with hundreds of employees. It all started with an idea that he acted on. He reminded everyone in that room that when you run into an opportunity, you MUST act on it or someone else will.

What if you don't want to start your own company? That's fine. Whatever you have as an aspiration or dream you are going to need to ACT on it. The first time I really acted on something like this was one of my investments.

I'm always investing in different things, but the

one that took a lot of commitment and research was my first property. I knew real estate lined up with my end goal of being financially free; I just hadn't pulled the trigger. I had done a lot of research online, spoke with relatives familiar about investing in real estate, and even spoke with some realtors that solely worked with investors. I had saved enough cash for two down payments in three years and still had not invested.

I was paralyzed. I had become my biggest roadblock! Not because I didn't have a proper understanding to get started or that I didn't have the cash; I was mentally stuck on the edge of the cliff of making a life changing decision. I was AFRAID. I was dreaming and knew what my long-term goals were, but I wasn't ACTING on them. I was being slapped in the face with an obvious answer but was ignoring it because I was afraid of the unknown. Seriously?! Was fear going to be the reason for my goal of financial freedom to slip farther away? No way!

So after I had already taken the small steps to expand my knowledge (and comfort zone) by researching and pulling together my funds, it was time to take the calculated risk. After finding the realtor I was going to work with and the property manager to handle the homes while I was out of state, we found the first property and put in an offer.

After all that time, I realized I could have shaved a solid two years off of my decision. I was the kid on the highest diving board holding up the line because I was too afraid to jump. If I could do it again and have the chance to start over, I would have pulled the trigger sooner only because I had done all the research and intelligence gathering I could…all I needed to do was jump into ACTion.

SO WHAT DOES THIS MEAN TO YOU?

…Ideas…
…Thoughts…
…Dreams…
… are all unrealized; just feelings floating around in our heads. It could be the best thing since sliced bread (always seems to be where we place the bar), but it isn't real until you make it so. I'm writing this while I am also acting on an idea of mine. For so long, I thought about writing, but never really acted on it. I've been awakened at night with brilliant ideas, wrote them down, and never acted on them. Have you ever had something creep into your mind that you're convinced is a good idea, and nothing ever comes of it? Did those ideas ever make it out of your head? You know what the difference is between that and some of the most successful entrepreneurs in the world?

Say it out loud! They took ACTion! THEY TOOK THE FIRST STEP!

"They" are the entrepreneurs, the doers, and the people we read about in TIME. Those that have succeeded acted on those thoughts, dreams, and ideas to make them a reality. YES, they have failed, sometimes multiple times, but it is the sole fact that they acted on the idea that separates them from you and me. It took me almost four years to realize that I was thinking of some great ideas, but never acted on them. Don't fall into the trap that everyone else, including myself, does!

Keep your mind open to problems that haven't been solved, to questions left unanswered, and think of a solution. Is there a problem at work? Do you have thoughts of an idea that could solve a significant problem? Have you acted on any of them? Do yourself a favor and ACT on your idea today and bask in the enjoyment of seeing what acting on a thought provides!

DAY 15 Completed: ____/____/_____

Write down some of your grandest ideas and dreams.

Have you acted on any of the ideas above? If not, what is your plan to do that this week?

What are you going to do to make sure you ACT on your dreams and ideas in the future?

What did this mean to you?

> *"It isn't what we say or think that defines us, but what we DO"*
>
> *– Jane Austen*

DAY 16

- THE DOUBLE EDGED SWORD -

Like the majority of Americans, I was raised in a middle-class family. My parents made sure to give us the best life possible with what little they had at the expense of credit card debt. As long as I can remember, I have consistently reminded myself to grow up having some money. I'd have so much money that I wouldn't be in the same situation my parents were in when I was younger. For me this was a unique thought because I had two very different influences when it came to my view of money. My father always said that "money makes the world go round," while my mother always reminded me that "money isn't everything and can't make you happy." Two relatively negative views, I believe, on what money can provide for someone. These are both common sayings and yet aren't entirely accurate.

In your 20s, you lean towards the former, or my dad's opinion in this case, realizing that money means power in our world. My thoughts were no different. I relentlessly worked 60 hours a week on a slow week for my first three years out of college. This included sacrificing time with my family, my little brother, potentially long-term relationships, and even my personal time. I worked weekends in different states and traveled in airports when most people were at home or sleeping. If you ever feel the need to try out being homeless, just miss your flight and stay in the airport overnight…bathing in a bathroom sink is an eye-opening experience.

I could see I had focused so much on a paycheck and was blinded by it. I could tell why my mom had called money a double-edged sword at this point. By focusing on working as hard as possible, just looking forward to the paycheck at the end of the week, and ultimately my new "lifestyle," I had forgotten some of the most important things in my life. I had missed birthdays of people close to me, I wasn't as happy at home (because I'd rather be making the next paycheck), and just forgot what was important to me. Money caused me to have some great experiences, but my desire for it had cut deeply into my emotional wellbeing. If you're forgetting to say happy birthday to someone that you're close to, forgetting what's vital in your life, and irritable with those that are supposedly your family, it might be time to reconsider your grip on that double-edged sword.

I gradually adjusted where my time was spent and over the years I have learned how to manage my personal and professional life. I now focus on keeping in touch with my family and friends more often. I try to make an effort to visit more often, and I take more time for myself, even if that meant taking a day off and escaping my cell phone. Although a paycheck helps stock my bachelor bare fridge, it's not just about a paycheck for me anymore. It's about appreciating what I have had the opportunity to earn and appreciating what I already have…including my family and friends.

SO WHAT DOES THIS MEAN TO YOU?

I'm not going to lie and say that making a good paycheck at a young age is going to make life hard. Money does make the world go round, and I still continue to work my ass off during the week. I still spend plenty of nights a week in hotels and the extra time is used for my personal ventures and investments.

The difference now is that I also understand money isn't everything. That means making time for people who are important to you, including yourself. Knowing this can make your life much more manageable.

Don't get me wrong. Focusing on developing your career and being "selfish" should be a priority as a young gun. Just don't forget that cash can be a double-edged sword and destroy some of the most precious things you used to care about before that paycheck. If you learn how to wield a double-edged sword (money in this case), you won't have to worry about getting stitches. When you close this book today, evaluate where you stand with your outlook on money, and see if you've noticed an impact on your life because of it.

DAY 16 Completed: ____/____/_____

What is your outlook on money?

If you had everything you wanted, would it change your outlook on money?

What can you do to positively impact the way you look at money today?

How can you ensure your outlook on money stays healthy and positive in the future?

What did this mean to you?

"Money has never made a man happy, nor will it, there is nothing in its nature to produce happiness. The more of it one has the more one wants."

– Benjamin Franklin

DAY 17

- PERSONAL DEVELOPMENT BUILDS NET WORTH -

It was too good to be true. I had made it into the top ten territories in the company, and my income began to reflect that. On top of that, I was being selected for a promotion and, to a career focused individual, upward mobility is always welcome. For most companies, a promotion means an increase in pay, benefits, less travel, etc. This was not the case for this particular opportunity, which I was offered at the end of 2013.

The new role being offered was a brand new position with less pay (with the potential to make more) and a lot more travel. It was a role where the select few were to coach their teams on how to sell a service that was struggling, and, to make it a little more challenging, the description of the role was still unknown. The service itself was a complicated genetic test, which could help a physician find the best med match for a patient.

We had the task of re-launching this service. The role itself was an experimental leadership role where we had to not only increase the medically necessary utilization of this genetic service but also learn how to share such a complicated service in a simple message. This is easier said than done, especially when you take a bunch of business professionals and tell them to educate others on something as complicated as genetics. I went to school for marketing and graduated with a Bachelors in Business Administration…can you see the challenge? The most in-depth science class I took was Anthropology.

I thought about the offer. After speaking with as many of my mentors and friends as I could, I knew I had to make the decision on my. Before 2015 had arrived, I decided I was going to accept the promotion to this new role. At first, I struggled with my decision because of the situation I placed myself in. I again chose to move to a new city to start over meeting new friends and ended up even farther from my family. That technically gave me three days a week to build a new life as a single 24-year-old. I had done that twice moving to Georgia and Los Angeles.

Now, as I look back, it was one of the best personal decisions of my life. The following two years provided me experiences that allowed me to grow personally and made up some of this book. Some of my greatest lessons learned were from managers, directors, friends, and even myself—all because I took a chance. With the help from some of my most respected mentors. I got the opportunity to mold the new role into something unique.

By definition, personal development is described as the activities that improve awareness and identity, develop talents and potential, build human capital and facilitate employability, enhance the quality of life, and contribute to the realization of dreams and aspirations. This is my favorite definition of personal development because it focuses on YOU and YOUR brand. Everything in that definition involves improving yourself, both mentally and physically, to contribute to the realization of your aspirations.

The key is that you have to give time to these activities to realize the benefits of personal development. The links to personal development and professional success are astounding. Google Oprah Winfrey, Michael Jordan, and Mark Cuban and see what they do for their development. All of these people spend time improving on their talents, potential, identity, and their overall human capital. It's so prevalent that Hal Elrod, a successful sales rep and coach, researched the most efficient, proven personal development practices used by top entrepreneurs in his book *The Miracle Morning*.

With this much correlation between personal development and one's personal/professional success, wouldn't you want to spend time each day devoting time to improving yourself? I'd say you do and that every day you should challenge yourself with this book; that's just the start.

SO WHAT DOES THIS MEAN TO YOU?

The quotes and sayings that promote personal development over anything else replayed in my mind for a very long time after I accepted the position. Primarily because I was so stuck on the pay cut, which wasn't that bad. I was just being the living embodiment of the spoiled millennial stereotype we've all come to accept. If you just keep an open mind and always remind yourself to do what's right for you, you'll quickly discover that personal development will be the most long-lasting investment you can find.

Money comes and goes, friends come and go, free time never stays the same, but your experience and the lessons life teaches you lives with you every day of your life. Your knowledge and expertise can be one of the most powerful tools you'll possess in your entire lifetime, and you can decide exactly how many tools you'll have!

Of course, personal development isn't just education by way of a book. It can be life reminding you how to live without worry or teach you to take every opportunity that comes your way. These lessons, dare I say "life lessons," mold you into the person that you grow to be. If you think that the only way to become "rich" and successful is to get a bigger paycheck, you might be slowing down your income. Greatness will follow if you just invest in yourself.

Growing your abilities and knowledge is an investment that only has a positive return on investment…you can't lose. Is there an opportunity that you're holding back on? Do you think it will help develop you as a person? Don't wait! Start to increase your net worth by chasing your personal development today.

DAY 17 Completed: ____/____/_____

Where do you think you could develop as a person?

What can you do today to develop as a person?

How are you going to ensure you're going develop in the future and continue to strive for personal development?

What did this mean to you?

"Income seldom exceeds personal development."

-Jim Rohn

DAY 18

- Y.O.L.O. (YOU ONLY LIVE ONCE) -

My first summer spent on two wheels was nothing short of exhilarating. The motorcycle season was coming to a close in Seattle, and by that I mean it was beginning to rain every single day. Since buying the donor-cycle during July 4th weekend, I had spent four months and 4,400 miles getting acquainted with my new hobby. I would have had a motorcycle much earlier than 2014 if I had anything to say about it, but I had a registered nurse as a mother and she didn't feel like seeing me in the hospital piecing me back together. Chicks dig scars, so I wouldn't have been opposed to a few more as a kid.

I was raised with the belief that motorcycles were two-wheeled death machines that provided organs for those in need. The nurses on my mother's floor called them donor-cycles. Sadly, it wasn't until a ride along with one of the reps in Northern California that my view of motorcycles had changed. In the position I held at the time I was writing this, I was allowed to ride with reps in different territories. My goal was to help sell our services and improve on the messaging we had crafted for our service.

By the time I had made it to this particular region, I had registered and canceled the motorcycle class three times. I had done my research, but I just couldn't figure out if I was being indecisive due to fear or if there was some legitimate danger in what I was going for.

The class was called "Motorcycle Safety Foundation Course," and it is required in the state of Washington to get a motorcycle endorsement. I don't remember how we got on the topic of two wheels, but it led one of the sales representatives to tell me a story about a family she was close with. The story was of a middle-class family that also lived in Northern California. The husband worked as a sales representative for a medical company. Their lives were just as you'd imagine an average nine to five family.

One morning the husband took the same highway he always traveled, and it had just as much traffic as any other California freeway. Everything seemed like a normal day until he found himself behind a truck carrying some metal pipes.

The rep was a little choked up here but continued with the best detail possible. Apparently, something came loose on the truck and sent a two-foot long pipe hurtling down the highway. The husband was not tailgating, but at 70 mph there isn't much room for adjustment. Out of sheer chance, the piece of pipe hit the highway and careened towards the husband's windshield. At just the right angle and speed, the pipe pierced the windshield and continued through the husband's chest. Shortly after it passed through the windshield, he crashed into an embankment. He left his wife and three children on this earth because of some freak accident. I'm confident he didn't wake up expecting that to happen.

Although a dark story, it should remind every single one of us of something we forget about. We only live once, and we can't take it for granted. It changed my mind on more than just getting a motorcycle, but reminded me to live every day to the fullest. By just saying yes to more experiences and having more of an open mind (as if it is my last day), I've had opportunities I never thought I would.

This book is a representation of the meaningful messages we receive every day that are guiding us and teaching us to live our best lives. Life comes at us extremely fast, and if we don't pay attention or think we have all the time in the world, we'll blink, and it'll all be over. This message is one of the most important ones in this book (and in my life) because by understanding that life is short, and every day counts, you begin to pay more attention to key aspects of your life—including you and your happiness. Remember, you only live once, so make it count.

SO WHAT DOES THIS MEAN TO YOU?

We all live like there is a tomorrow. We let fear drive our decisions. We tell ourselves we'll just do "blank" later. I'll change this tomorrow. I'll start eating right next week. I'll tell her I love her tonight. What if there isn't a tomorrow? The man in this story was a good guy with a normal job and a full family. He wasn't racing his car; he wasn't doing anything risky…just driving for work! He kissed his wife goodbye one last time and left to never return. What do you think he would have done differently if he knew he only had the next 24 hours? What would you do if you were only going to live for the next 24 hours?

I'm sure there are a lot of things you'd move up the priority list if you knew that small piece of information. Like the gentleman in the story, we are not privy to that, so you need keep in mind that tomorrow is not promised to you. I'm not saying to avoid planning for the future, but treat the present day as if it is your last. Are you still procrastinating on doing something? Something that you'd do if you knew you had limited time left? You only live once and time is running out…close this book and do it today!

DAY 18 Completed: ____/____/_____

What would you have done differently in the past 24 hours if you knew those would have been your last?

How are you going to treat today and tomorrow differently with that same mentality?

How will you remind yourself to really live each day like it's your last?

What did this mean to you?

"Everything you want is on the other side of fear."

-Jack Canfield

DAY 19

- NOT EVERYONE DRINKS THE SAME CUP OF TEA -

A visit to Pike Place Market in Seattle frequently results in a food coma and the possibility of getting run over by a manic shopper. People in the Northwest throw down harder than Rhonda Rousey for a good organic vegetable. This day was no different other than the fact I had one of my best friends, Brock, visiting from Florida. I had to make sure he saw the spots Seattle was known for. Becoming much more accustomed to spending time with friends, I made sure to take the Friday off to begin the tour I had perfected.

We started at a scooter shop, so Brock had his own ride. He was going to ride a scooter, and I would ride my motorcycle through some of the coolest spots in western Washington. It was either two wheels or walking because of how crazy parking was in the city and we decided on the former. One of our first stops was the fabulous Pike Place Market, where you can find jet-fuel infused coffee and the gut-wrenching smell of fish. We stopped here to grab some lunch after a busy morning seeing some of the tourist spots farther away from the city.

We went to an excellent restaurant called Lowells, and it was packed. The two-person bro date we had going on had commandeered one the largest tables in the restaurant. As our food was called, we locked eyes with two ladies that were also picking up their food. They were in a dangerous predicament with standing room only in the restaurant. They eyed our table and asked if they could share with us. I couldn't get away with saying no because we had the titanic of all tables.

At first, both parties focused on their food, but halfway into the meal I overheard something I couldn't ignore. It was an opportunity to jump into the conversation with some beautiful ladies. Brock was on one side of the table next to one of the girls, and I was on across from him. Come to find out the girls were sisters.

What was so interesting about the conversation I was having was how different we both were. She grew up in Eugene, Oregon and I grew up in Sanford, Florida. That alone could cause problems. If you don't believe me, spend a few months in Sanford. The people of the South tend to be a little more close-minded to a lot of social norms accepted on the West Coast.

We discovered how I loved anything that got the adrenaline pumping, while she was the exact opposite. She preferred a book and some quiet time—it makes me anxious just thinking about being still long enough to finish lunch. We continued to text back and forth for a few weeks, and then the mutual interest fizzled out.

By just learning to keep an open mind and listen to what this girl was saying allowed me to be engaged in the conversation and have fun at that casual lunch. I'm using this example, but this can be said for any day you're out, and someone starts talking about something you don't know about, care about, or are completely against. Let's say you're at meeting with some key decision makers for a product you're pushing, and the boss says something you completely disagree with. If you can't push through that, you might end up with a missed opportunity. An opportunity to sell in that case, but really by closing off your mind after disagreeing, you're ultimately closing off any chances of an opportunity life could present to you.

SO WHAT DOES THIS MEAN TO YOU?

I understood the importance of what this girl unknowingly taught me, and what I'll share with you, only after I looked back through my writing.

I was attracted to her physically, which got my attention and forced me to explore further. We started to get to know each other and quickly found out we were far too different. It was like someone was telling her to dislike everything I said. We almost didn't make it past the point of "I don't like motorcycles." In all honesty, what talking with her did was make me realize (and retain the fact) that not everything is for everybody. Ever heard the saying "that's not my cup of tea"? Well, your grandma was right and what she meant by that was that everyone likes and dislikes different things.

By keeping an open mind in this world, you can connect with common interests and build a relationship with many more people. Of course, there are issues and personal morals where you won't compromise, and that's okay. Be honest with yourself here. Do you like everything your best friend likes? What about your mom? Girlfriend? Husband?

No. No way.

Understanding that everyone likes different things and being open to hearing them takes a conversation from "we're done here" to "tell me more"! All of a sudden that "tell me more" can turn in to an opportunity in the form of a new business partner, relationship, another connection, or just the friend who will support you in the future. Today, try your best to keep an open mind with everyone you talk to and understand that not everything is for everyone. Don't turn off your ears because you disagree. You might learn something or, better yet, get a phone number!

DAY 19 Completed: ____/____/_____

When have you had such a disagreement with someone that you immediately stopped listening?

If you had kept more of an open mind, would the outcome above be any different? Do you think there was a missed opportunity?

What are you going to do to make sure you stay open-minded today?

How are you going to make sure you stay more open-minded in the future?

What did this mean to you?

"Be kind. Be friendly. Be likeable. But don't worry if somebody doesn't like you. You won't be everybody's cup of tea, and that's okay. You can be somebody's cup of coffee, instead, and coffee is AWESOME"

– L.R. Knost

DAY 20

- DROP THE VELVET HAMMER -

When someone in sales says that they've had a terrible week, it most likely was so stress inducing that a mere mortal would not have survived. Not only do we face a work week that never ends (because our phones never shut off in sales), but we also deal with constant terminations of team members, cuts to our pay if we missed quota, never ending change with our current clients, and, the most feared of all, rejection. I knew a team that was finishing up a week like that. They had to terminate someone from their team, and I felt it could have been done differently.

The biggest cause of the termination, as is with any sales job, is the lack of new business. As a manager and leader, your job is to dig deeper and find out what the problem is instead of just firing the employee. You probe until the employee gives you the underlying problem and you attempt to fix it, or you realize that the employment isn't going to work out. The situation the team was facing was the latter. To be honest, it was much more often the latter than anything else. From my point of view, this wasn't the hardest part in this particular situation.

It was the fact that there were warning signs. You could tell something was up, but the team was not as direct as they needed to be. When they thought they were out of time, all of the team came together and had a meeting with this particular employee. The idea was to meet and set a plan to hopefully save them. Unfortunately, the meeting was not received well by said employee, and it started to go downhill from there. What already was apparent in the lack of work ethic and new business became even more prevalent.

Although they agreed to the plan the team set for them, internally they had already given up on working and had become defensive. I feel that if the team had confronted them earlier and the employee would have just asked for help, the result would have been much different. I understood what happened, why they had the meeting and what the result was, but this lesson didn't hit home until I was on the receiving end of something like this.

Shortly after we let this employee go, I ended up receiving the same treatment at a meeting. I had a taste of my own medicine and damn did it taste bad.

I had just finished a presentation with our managed markets team to an insurance company. The sales force will attend these types of meetings to secure contracts to make sure the particular insurances pay us. These can be some of the most challenging meetings for a medical salesperson because they are typically stacked with people that specialize in what they do (in this case a PhD level pharmacist) and the meetings also have a much bigger focus on cost. When I walked out and finished that meeting, I felt I did amazing. I sold what our company does best and answered every question to the best of my ability. It was one of the moments where no matter what someone says, you have the best response. So after the meeting, the managed markets team went on their way, and I thought that was it.

A few weeks later, found out what managed

markets thought of the meeting. "Completely bombed" were the words used in the review. I was frustrated and a little annoyed, but this instantaneously burned the lesson into my mind. If something is said incorrectly, gracefully correct it. If you see someone do something that impacts somebody negatively, say something about it. Someone cannot improve on how they respond to situations and react to confrontation if the observer never gives any criticism or advice.

SO WHAT DOES THIS MEAN TO YOU?

DROP THE HAMMER!

Tell it like it is! It might not sound great or give you that warm and fuzzy feeling, but it needs to get done. If you take one thing from these two stories, remember to be direct and upfront with your critiques, emotions, or whatever else might be plaguing you. Why?

If you don't, they come back to haunt you. Maybe not directly, but through experiences, you get to clean up. The team that let the salesperson go without initially addressing specific issues spent months fixing the problems left behind. This can be even more important as a leader in any situation because you have people looking to you for advice and they respect you for what you know. Now being rude and being candid can be two different things. You can gracefully share what your opinions or emotions are without being rude or condescending. By smoothly hitting someone with the truth, there's a much greater chance that they'll be receptive and not defensive.

So what happens when you hold an emotion in? It all just builds up and can make you sick (physically and mentally); nothing gets fixed and, worst of all, you might let all that pent up frustration out on the wrong person. Why risk all of that?

Do yourself, and everyone around you, a favor by gracefully telling it like it is or in this case, dropping the velvet hammer…I'm sure there is something you'd like to share today.

DAY 20 Completed: ____/____/_____

What are three things you have on your mind that you really need to share with someone? Why haven't you done it?

How are you going to make sure you stay as candid as possible with everyone you talk to this week?

How will you keep up candid communication in the future?

What did this mean to you?

> "Good communication is just as stimulating as black coffee and just as hard to sleep after"
> - Anne Morrow Lindbergh

DAY 21

- DO A DOUBLE TAKE -

For 455 days, I had to endure physical torture by way of plastic retainers. The orthodontists called them "Invisalign trays," but most people would choose to describe them as oral cruelty. For those blessed with never having braces or Invisalign, a tray is a "set" of molds of your teeth you wear for a total of two weeks at a time. You swap out your old tray and move onto the new one at the end of that two-week period. Eventually, I got used to the pain of moving teeth, dealing with them in my mouth, and constantly having to brush my teeth. But not before my fair share of annoyances. Like anything in this world, it was getting started that was the biggest challenge for me.

I didn't know much about Invisalign and primarily listened to my orthodontist (the guy trying to sell me on them). My bite was more of the issue than the alignment of my teeth, but insurance covered it and I could finally afford it. I agreed to the treatment and within the first 48 hours realized there were a few details the doc left out.

After about two weeks, I was ready to throw in the towel. I had to change the way I ate, when I ate, how often I brushed my teeth, and even what I could drink! I was limited to water with the trays in my mouth. How often during the day do you drink something other than water?! It CHANGED my lifestyle for the entire time they were in my mouth. I brushed after every meal or snack; they had to be in 22 hours out of the day, and my risk of cavities increased if I didn't follow the first two steps. I wasn't ready for that, especially for such minor improvements to my mouth.

What was even more frustrating was the fact that a salesperson I worked with the week before I got them was also thinking about getting Invisalign. He knew so much more than I did and seemed as if this was his second time around getting braces. Did he have a better doctor? No. He merely listened to more than just the doctor and did his research. If I had taken some of my own time to study the most common things about Invisalign, I could have avoided a lot of stress and anxiety caused by the little devices.

So why am I sharing my story about ortho treatment? It has nothing to with treatment itself but the results of my lack of research and due diligence. It's just like signing a contract without reading it through or having an attorney do so. If you don't do your due diligence and sign, there might be a nasty surprise waiting for you in the fine print of a contract. From this point forward, although a little cynical, I ask myself what isn't being presented or questioned. It allows me to think through a lot of my decisions instead of just impulsively diving at a response.

SO WHAT DOES THIS MEAN TO YOU?

How many times have you said to yourself "I wish I knew that before I did blank"? This is just the next step in being decisive but not impulsive. I try my hardest now to do my own research, whether or not I've already got somebody else's opinions. You make hundreds of decisions every single day, so why would you let someone else tell you what to do? Yes, hearing an opinion from an expert is always great and extremely useful, BUT those views are sometimes biased and not objective. Not only that, but NO one is always right. Remember, the only guaranteed thing in life is taxes and death, not an "expert's" opinion.

This isn't something you can use for just your next orthodontic treatment, but for anything you do during your time on earth! Buying a car, a house, or any other large investment of your personal time and hard earned money deserves some of your dedicated time to research. Do some of your own research and you'll find yourself saving a ton of time and avoiding unneeded stress. Doing a double-take is never a bad thing; you're just making sure everything checks out.

DAY 21 Completed: ____/____/_____

Write down something that would have had a different outcome if you would have just done your own due diligence.

What's a big decision coming up that you need to do some research on? When are you are going to do that research this week?

Why will you continue to do your due diligence on future endeavors?

What did this mean to you?

"Diligence is the Mother of good fortune"

– Benjamin Disraeli

DAY 22

- WHAT ARE YOU WORTH -

Before spending time in a sales role, I thought being in leadership meant a simpler way of life. You'd come into work and "manage" your team. You'd sit in your nice office, looking through numbers and paperwork, while your team busted their asses for much less pay. I discovered that a leadership role at the company I joined was far different. The sales managers in my business were in the trenches with you, fighting along side you, and (most of the time) working longer hours than you.

When I finally had the opportunity to team up with the regional manager and director of the West Coast I realized that what goes on behind the scenes, as leadership in a company, is far more intense than I first thought. And that was with the limited view I had. I spent some time with both the director and regional vice president on my personal ability to coach and lead, and one thing that I honestly struggled with was finding my worth on each ride along*.

So if they didn't need help selling, what value was I bringing to the field when I rode with the sales rep in each territory? I couldn't find an answer, and that was my problem! The director leveled with me on our next coaching session and shared she had the same problem going into the leadership role. She shared the two things that helped her push through that personal challenge. First, she found out what she felt she did well. Something that stood out from just being "persistent" or "ambitious," which are both common buzzwords in regards to sales. What were her strengths that separated her from everyone else? I needed to understand my basic strengths and answer this exact question for myself.

---

* Like I mentioned earlier in this book, a ride along is when someone in a leadership role spends time coaching and selling with sales people in the field.

Second, she thought about what she could do to make here sales representatives lives easier before each field ride along. Not only was she bringing value with her personal strengths, but she was doing what only the most successful managers and directors do… problem-solving. She went to every field with the goal of solving some problems for the reps in that territory and removing obstacles for the territory.

With this direction, I found I was bringing value with my own personal strengths, I just needed to realize it. I was creative and by containing that to my personal life was just slowing me down. Using those strengths, I was able to make every field ride more productive and found that I became more of a resource to the reps than I was before. Even if they were more than competent to sell our service or better in a specific situation than me, I felt I was still able to make an impact with some of the problems we faced in the field.

This was important to me not just because it allowed me to confidently feel I brought value to my team, but that I could actively look at a situation and understand exactly where I fit in. Earlier, we talked about knowing your value in a team setting and this is a perfect way to do that. By knowing what I excelled at and what fixed variable I offered to people around me, I felt valuable to my team.

A growing body of research (found in the Harvard Business Review), including new studies by Berkeley's Juliana Breines and Serena Chen, insinuate that self-compassion, instead of self-esteem, could be the key to unlocking your true potential. So what does that have to do with anything here? Self-compassion is, by definition, a willingness to look at your mistakes and shortcomings with kindness and understanding — it's embracing the fact that to slip up is human nature. This is half the battle of finding exactly where you are valuable to you friends, your family, your coworkers, and your team. By looking at your shortcomings mistakes and in this case your strengths with understanding, you can focus on your strengths, your value, and share that openly with those in need.

SO WHAT DOES THIS MEAN TO YOU?

If you do more than just drag through the day like a retiree in Florida, then you've probably asked yourself…

"What is my value?"

I know I would and still do! It proves you're situationally aware and have a level of emotional intelligence that some people lack. What this story means to you is that you can start making an impact in your life by finding out how you have affected the world around you. What are you known for? What do your friends and family call on you for? These could be perfect examples of what you excel at without you even knowing.

If you dig, you'll find that you impacted them with a strength or ability of your own that they did not possess. EVERYONE has value to bring to this earth; it just depends on whether or not you realize your potential and what you offer! Today, think carefully about what makes you different from your best friend, significant other, and family members…today, realize your worth!

DAY 22 Completed: ____/____/_____

What are some things that make you unique?

EVERYONE has value. What are the ways you're going to share yours today?

What have you done this week to share your worth? How will you continue to do so?

What did this mean to you?

"If you don't know your own worth and value, don't expect someone else to calculate it for you"

– Unknown

DAY 23

- DON'T GO INVISIBLE -

Summer had finally arrived in Seattle, and I was still in a coat. I wasn't surprised and had come to accept the fact that warm outerwear had become part of my year-round wardrobe. I was meeting with Nicole, who had been a friend, mentor, and coach since my collegiate years. I had not had a chance to sit down with Nicole in some time, and I was looking forward to it. She had this tendency to capitalize on every opportunity to empower and develop the people around her: not just employees but friends and family…a real leader in every form of the word.

One thing Nicole did particularly well was turn any moment you spent with her, a conversation in this case, into a learning experience. She was so good at this that I never had a coaching scenario with her where I didn't have that "AHA!"

moment.

This time we started talking about how I was doing with communicating with my team. I proceeded to explain how good things were and where I felt my communication was with the team. After going back and forth about the different territories, she started questioning she started questioning who else I was communicating with on a regular basis. At this point in the conversation, I was trying to figure out what I could be doing better and where we were going with this. Nicole doesn't just ask a question to hear herself speak, there is purpose to it…

She then asked who I *should* be communicating with. I listed my reps, my manager, my director, and a few others in leadership… "Aha!" I think I knew where she was going with this. Nicole took a piece of paper and started drawing a chart where I was the middle (along with my peers), with the sales reps and upper management around me.

She continued to explain how my networking shouldn't stop at those on my team. I needed to network with the VP's, people at the home office, my peers, and others that could impact my day-to-day work. I merely needed to stay visible within the company as a whole. It was more than just networking, but building a relationship for a time when you might need to utilize them for more than just friendship.

Not only did she open my eyes to the fact that I was doing a horrible job at keeping in touch with my coworkers, but I did a pretty bad job at this in general. Although by this point in my life I had become better at keeping in touch with those in my immediate circle (close friends and family), I was still lacking in keeping my network alive. For my work life, I chose a few people that Nicole and I talked about that day and made an effort, throughout the week, to reach out to them with questions, resources, and even ideas. Then after they became part of my weekly calls, I moved on to others.

For my personal life, I chose to go through social media and find someone I hadn't talked to in a while and reach out through a call, a text, or a Facebook message just to catch up. It's been fun being able to reminisce and see where a lot of my old friends and family members I've lost contact with were at. On top of that, I kept the one thing that a person has for their entire life intact and alive: my personal network of contacts and relationships.

Cultivating your professional and personal network can be stronger than you think or that I can show here. In a study done in 1998 at the University of Pennsylvania, sociologist Randall Collins showed that breakthroughs from icons such as the seven sages of antiquity, Freud, Picasso, Watson and Crick, and Pythagoras were the consequence of a personal network that prompted their individuality.

The only three exceptions Collins could find in all of recorded history were Taoist Wang Chung, Bassui Tokusho, and Ibn Khaldun. What this says is that building a diverse network (and keeping it alive by communicating with those contacts) cannot only positively impact your personal life, but your professional career as well! History is backing this one up.

SO WHAT DOES THIS MEAN TO YOU?

This is "Business 101" that isn't taught in any college or high school.

Can you think of that one person who knows everyone and reaches out all the time? That guy or girl that you don't mind talking to at the end of a long work day. They always seem to take a genuine interest in whatever is going on in your life.

Even when they don't need anything, you've heard from them. They don't always want something or need your help, but when they do are you more willing to help? Of course you are!

Why is that? Why do we work with this person compared to the random call from a high school friend for help with rent? Because you know the former! It feels as if you have a relationship outside the normal "mooching" friend. This isn't just about asking favors; it's about building a smart professional and personal network. A lot of the time moving up in the world or getting where you need to be to reach your goals requires knowing the right people. Of course, that network you build, like anything else worth having, requires maintenance. In this case, staying visible in your network is the maintenance required.

Staying visible in your company, within your group of friends, and even in your family is something that your future self will thank you for. You'll never be the mooching friend or the person who just calls when they need something. You'll just be the smart one utilizing your well-maintained social network. Make the effort today to improve your visibility within your personal and professional network by reaching out to someone you know you need to talk with.

DAY 23 Completed: ____/____/_____

Who do you NEED to reach out to? When was the last time you talked to them and why?

How can you build your network this week?

How will you continue to do so?

What did this mean to you?

> "Always stay on the bridge between the invisible and visible"
>
> – Paulo Coelho

DAY 24

- MAX OUT YOU MENTAL 401(K) -

Although I did take some time to invest in my future, by the time I was 22 I had fallen into the materialistic black hole that so many people had done before me. My money was spent on things that provided that short-term feeling of pleasure. Cars, watches, and clothes all became a financial vacuum. It wasn't until I began to spend my hard earned cash on experiences rather than materials before I realized investments are not just made for the stock market and your 401(k), but your mental health.

There was a trend I found when I began to invest in my fulfilling adventures. Taking time off of work to travel overseas and do the running of the bulls left me with a feeling of being so much smaller compared to how big this world is. I learned how to ride, race, and maintain a motorcycle instead of buying the most expensive one out there. I learned how to play an instrument at 26 because it was something I wanted to pass to my children (the guitar is also a blast to play!). All of these cost me a price, both time and money, but the long-term memory and enjoyment they brought will never fade away.

The trend was in how I felt after each adventure compared to how I felt when I bought a new car or the newest GoPro. The toys brought me a short-term feeling of enjoyment that slowly faded. Sadly, this is how most of us live. We think that buying the next toy is going to make us happy. It DOES, but for a short time. After a while, they didn't excite me as they did when I first got them, and eventually I wanted something new. The adventures and experiences I had were different. It was a spike in pleasure with repeated jumps in happiness for as long as I could remember them, which as long as I avoid memory loss I'll have them for the rest of my life.

Now don't get me wrong. I'm not saying that I have completely forgotten about the materialistic things in my life. Because of my love for anything with a motor, I'll continue to invest my time and money into the financial pitfalls that motorized vehicles are. What I'm saying is that invest in how makes you happy in the long-term. The majority of that time that feeling is correlated to an "experience" like a vacation or racing a car.

Again, this isn't just my personal observation; it's backed by numerous studies. One of which, conducted by Ryan Howell, assistant professor of psychology at San Francisco State University. Howell looked at 154 people enrolled at San Francisco State University with an average age of about 25. Those included in the study answered questions about a recent purchase personally made in the last three months with the intention of making themselves happy.

While most were happy with their purchase, those who shared information about experiences tended to show a higher satisfaction at the time and after the experience had passed. The biggest difference was in how participants said others around them reacted to either the purchased object or experience. Experiences led to more happiness in others than purchases did. A sense of relatedness to others may be one of the reasons why experiences generate more happiness.

The common theme here is what your experience/purchase ends up making you feel. I learned to look at my purchases (experiences/cars/etc.) and evaluate whether or not they were worth it. Will it make me happy for the short-term? The long-term? Is it something I'll never forget.

SO WHAT DOES THIS MEAN TO YOU?

Not only do our past experiences shape who we are when we grow and develop, but those experiences form memories that last a lifetime. If you're lucky, you had some exquisite photos taken as well and, in that case, they'll last generations to come.

Now think about a positive memory from your childhood that you can't seem to shake.

Can you remember all the material things in that memory? Maybe.

Can you remember how much money you had? Probably not. Also, an allowance isn't something to get excited about.

Can you remember how you felt? Hell yes!

That feeling of joy, adrenaline, pain, and happiness all resurface. These experiences in your early life CREATE the person you become. Why do so many people finally feel like adults by their 30s? Because by 30-years-old, you've experienced 80% of what makes you who you are! Do you want to waste all your precious time on materialistic things that might not impact who you are down the road?

Experiences are something that stay with you and are mental investments for a day you need to pull out a positive memory and smile. So many people worry about maxing out their 401(k)s but forget about investing in themselves. When you're done with this book for today, think about an adventure or experience you've wanted to do. Sign up for it, plan for it, and, if you can, DO it today!

DAY 24 Completed: ____/____/_____

Write down some adventures you'd like to go on.

Pick one of those and figure out when you'll do it this next year.

How are you going to make sure you continue this mindset?

What did this mean to you?

> "What you do today is important because you are exchanging a day of your life for it"
>
> – Unknown

DAY 25

- JUSTIFY BEING A RISK TAKER -

In 2015, I lost $12,000 in the stock market in two transactions. Within a week, the stocks tumbled to a low that hadn't been seen since 2006. The prices hit my personal number to pull out, and I realized that loss. I'm sure this story sounds familiar to most investors that play in the market on their own...only 20% of average investors do better than the market as a whole. I was averaging 9% returns before this loss, and this took me into the red. Of course, 2015 was also the year I broke into real estate and purchased two turnkey* properties that turned a profit.

---

* A turnkey property is a home or apt ready to be immediately rented out.

What was the difference between the realized gain and the realized loss? Although one was much more painful for me, the difference I want to recognize is that one decision was made through impulsive decision making and the other through calculated analysis. I said a few chapters earlier that I have always had problems being impulsive and this stock market loss was an eye opener. Losing $12,000 because of your choices has the same shock factor as jumping into an ice-cold pool…not enjoyable, but it WAKES you up.

Since I had the ability to make my own decision and clearly communicate it, I have been impulsive. I'd let emotions run my indecisive choices. Does this story remind you of another one from earlier in the book? I hope so. The time I lost this amount in the stock market was the same time I signed up for Invisalign. I went with speculation when I lost that $12,000. This knee-jerk reaction could be seen in my relationships and other lost opportunities.

So after years of impulsive behavior and the rather painful mental and financial consequences, I was started on the road to change. With the help of a close friend and coach, I began changing my work environment. Instead of jumping at an answer or something an employee had a question on, I'd probe. I'd do my research, and I'd pull my information together to decide. Once I made my decision, I was committed. When I started to consciously control this in my working environment, it began to bleed into my everyday decisions. It was life changing.

When I finally had to decide on investing in profitable real estate investments, I took what I had changed in my personal behavior and attacked my real estate portfolio the same way. I was decisive, yet did my research and justified my risks with analysis and numbers showing the data would work out in my favor. It also really helped to have a competent realtor and property manager on your side. This story lines up with the story on Invisalign as well because they both have something to do with doing your due diligence and taking the jump. When I failed to do research on Invisalign, I ended up paying for it. When I based my stock market picks off of speculation, I lost money. It was obviously time for a change. It's easy to justify taking a risk, whether financially or personally, if you've just done your due diligence. If you're prepared, then don't freak yourself out; you've justified the risk. Do it!

SO WHAT DOES THIS MEAN TO YOU?

Google the number one reason real estate investors fail. Although there will be numerous answers, one stands out above all else…the inability to analyze one's property and manage it correctly. By jumping into an investment like real estate without examining the numbers, which is impulsive, the investors ultimately fail! Like the average real estate investor, my impulsive nature resulted in failure in my stock market ventures.

When I started adding a little more thought and logic to my decision process, good investments became great. I began to place logic and calculated risk into my everyday life, and I quickly found the way I made decisions began to impact my personal life!

Now, I still think with my heart and wear it as a shoulder ornament (it looks good there on my sleeve). I'm easily excited and as expressive as I've always been. I still have emotions like every other human being, yet after enough financial loss and pain from those horrid Invisalign trays, I've learned to control them. Learn from my mistakes and avoid that altogether.

I'm not saying you need to get into the real estate market.

I'm not telling you that being impulsive makes you an evil person. I'm sharing with you the difference it can make between being impulsive or taking a calculated risk. So here's the challenge…

Try not diving at your next answer to a question, argument, or significant decision. If you're on the opposite side of the equation and take months to decide, speed up the process by committing to your research and analysis. Find the happy middle ground and see how it improves your personal life and your investments. Today, justify being that calculated risk taker!

DAY 25 Completed: ____/____/_____

Where is opportunity hiding as risk in your life?

How are you going to justify taking that risk or not?

What's your plan to continue taking calculated risks?

What did this mean to you?

"Often the difference between a successful person and a failure is not one has better abilities or ideas, but the courage that one has to bet on one's ideas, to take a calculated risk — and to act"

- Andre Malraux

DAY 26

- TRANSPARENCY GAINS TRUST -

How many times were you told as a kid that "it'll be okay"? "Don't worry everything will be alright!" It's our nature as human beings to console those in emotional distress, so I'm sure this happened to you plenty of times, but did it change how you felt? Maybe, but most of the time you were still feeling uneasy, anxious, or both. Why? Because most of the time, the person trying to relax you isn't being transparent and completely honest with you. Either because they don't know what's happening or don't want to tell you 'the truth' to avoid any unwanted emotions.

The lack of transparency can create a sense of a muddled unknown. Think that's a healthy feeling? How would you feel if some guy in an alley in New York cooked you a meal and said, "just trust me, it'll be great"? Other than the feeling of nausea and something similar to irritable bowel syndrome, you'd most likely feel uneasy about the situation. Vivid picture I know, but that uneasy, nauseous feeling can develop when you know you're dealing with someone that is not being transparent.

I had the opportunity to test this theory while looking for a new investment. While living in Washington, the lack of transparency in a deal completely turned me away from an investment that could have been rather lucrative. I covered a large area including Northern California. One of the people I had befriended offered up an opportunity to begin investing in the legal growing of marijuana in Northern California. The idea was to purchase land, receive rent, and let the growers do their thing. It allowed us to be invested in a skyrocketing industry without having to do much. For me, there were too many unknowns.

I didn't know who was growing, where our target market was going to be, who would buy the licenses, and, most importantly, how we would secure our portion of the rent. How did I know what my return on investment was going to be? No one had an answer for me and instead they just tried to pull my emotional strings. "The industry was blowing up, and we could make millions," they kept saying…

It left me with an uneasy feeling and, based off of my research, there were key components not being mentioned from a few of the investors. I pulled the ripcord, without burning any bridges, and never looked back.

What if I knew more about the components essential to the deal? I might have invested. This is just an investment I'm talking about here, but, in all reality, a lack of transparency can impact your daily life a lot more than you think. Transparency is the foundation for trust. By being transparent, I've been able to show, by my actions, that I'm not hiding anything. There are no ill-intentions to what I do or hidden agendas when I work.

What this has done is allow friends, family, and clients to trust in what I say and do. For example, by being as transparent as possible in all of my sales calls, my clients are much more open to trusting me. That just means the next time I bring up a new service or product, the conversation doesn't revolve around them questioning the legitimacy of what I'm selling but the logistics of integrating into their practice.

A good example of this is when a car sales rep only says positive things about the car he or she is trying to sell. What happens is you forget to ask the right questions, then find out all the negatives to the car (unless you've done your due diligence) when you drive it home. Now you've created a horrible image of car sales people in your mind, and you don't trust the guy or girl that just sold you the car. Most people have experienced or know someone who has experienced the above example. After you think about that, you can't say that transparency doesn't gain trust.

SO WHAT DOES THIS MEAN TO YOU?

The unknown causes chaos and fear. It leaves people to their own imagination, and you know how crazy some people can be. What is the easiest way to solve that "unknown" feeling? By being honest and transparent. Just like Mother Teresa says. It makes you vulnerable, but you have a lot more to gain from it. This has to do with every facet of your life.

What happens at dinner when the menu doesn't have a description of what's in an entrée? We end up asking the server, and they gladly share what's hiding in the fancy dish on the menu. THEN we make our decision. The menu and server were honest, allowing us to make an educated decision. How would you feel if they told you some of the ingredients in the plate then received a surprised when they brought it out? Upset? Betrayed? Maybe dead if you're allergic to peanuts, and they didn't feel like sharing that. This is just a simple example, but can you see where honesty and transparency can impact you?!

Think of a situation where someone wasn't as transparent or honest with you. Was it a big decision? Did it change the way you felt about that person? If you say no, then you're lying. It destroys the trust they had built with you and can alter your relationship. Don't be the person that people don't believe. Try to be as transparent as possible when something is wrong, right, and everything in between. You'll be seen as a trustworthy person that tells it how it is and will be known for getting a straight answer. I'm sure there is a hard conversation you need to have with someone in your life. What are you waiting for? Go get transparent.

DAY 26 Completed: ____/____/_____

When have you avoided being transparent this week? What was the outcome?

How are you going to make sure you maintain honesty and transparency?

How will you push yourself to maintain transparency in the future?

What did this mean to you?

"Honesty and transparency make you vulnerable. Be honest and transparent anyway"

– Mother Teresa

DAY 27

- PLAN B WAS CREATED
FOR A REASON -

One of the hardest things to understand when I sat down with my first financial advisor out of college was one of the easiest things to do…build up an emergency fund. For those of you who aren't familiar with the term, it's just a rainy day fund; an easily liquidated pile of cash stored somewhere for one to gain access to for emergencies. These emergencies could be as simple as a broken down car that requires a large sum of money or something more severe like a lost job.

I didn't have a hard time grasping the process of creating one. All I needed to do was open up an account (Ally was and is great because they have a higher interest rate than most brick and mortar banks—for a savings account that is) and start socking away some of my money. It was the concept of having money; sitting in a low-interest savings account for the chance something bad might happen. It's hard to prep for the worst if the worst in college is not having too much in the fridge. Unfortunately, shortly after starting my career in sales in 2011, I had two friends show me the importance of a plan B or, in this case, an emergency fund.

Both of these friends were raised in middle-class families and had the opportunity to attend college. I was fortunate enough to meet both in college at the University of Central Florida and got to know both relatively well. After I had spent some time out in the field and was finally transferred to Los Angeles in 2012, I got a chance to speak with both of them. Both friends had lost the jobs they originally had and were looking for their second job out of college, which happens more often than not for a college graduate. Hell, a college graduate finding a job in the first place is a miracle nowadays. Although both were in similar situations, their preparation for something like this was glaringly obvious. Finally, what my financial advisor had said was starting to make sense.

My less prepared friend, with no savings for an emergency, was much more emotionally distraught and seriously stressed out. It made me double-check my bank account and my plan B. Was my financial backup plan strong enough? Could I survive an "emergency"? What happened if I lost my job today? These questions all became a reality for my buddy, and the answers were not ideal. They were caught with their proverbial pants down. In a way, they were lucky too. because they were single with no kids. Imagine having a family, a mortgage, closing on a home, a child on the way, or any other blessing life brings about. What if the emergency takes away the financial support for the things you want to spend your money on?

Life really can seem unfair unless you're prepped for it, which is a perfect segway into my other collegiate friend who had saved for plan B. This particular buddy was in the same situation, but due to preparation he was much less stressed. They almost had a positive attitude about the whole situation (which I have to commend in a situation like that). They knew that money doesn't last forever and because of that, they had started prepping for the worse. A plan B.

This taught me that life doesn't pick favorites. Some of the worst situations happen to the nicest, most sincere people. In the end, when you have a personal emergency, it doesn't matter how nice you are or if you're everyone's best friend. What is important is if you have a financial back-up plan for the worst case scenario. I've had to withdraw money a few times from my personal emergency fund for times where I was low on liquid cash or didn't want to put anything on a credit card. I'd immediately fill it back up with my next couple of paychecks and then leave it be. This was a powerful lesson that was forced on me and one I plan to pass along to my family. Prepare for the worst and hope for the best!

SO WHAT DOES THIS MEAN TO YOU?

Born in raised in Florida allowed me to become acquainted with tropical storms and hurricanes. Massive storms with winds that could blow trees out of the ground and flip cars. Even during hurricane season, most Floridians didn't care. Why? Because they had a backup plan!

The prepared had gas and an electrical generator when the power was knocked out, plenty of extra water, and non-perishable foods. Those that were ready for the disaster enjoyed grilled chicken after the storm passed without electricity, while others were rushing to the grocery store (where there wasn't any food or power). Think of your emergency fund, backup plan, plan B, or whatever you want to call it as your hurricane preparation kit.

So are you ready?

If something life altering happened tomorrow could you hack it?

Will you keep living day to day and not stress knowing everything will be alright?

Most of the working class can't give a resounding yes to that. For starters, a national survey shows that 63% of people said they don't have the savings to cover a $500 car repair and only four in ten Americans would be able to rely on savings to cover anything beyond their usual bills. The Federal Reserve took it a step further and compared it to income. According to the survey, the people most prepared for an emergency are the ones with incomes over $75,000 or a college education. Even with a higher income, 46% said they couldn't pay a $500 car repair. What? How is that even possible?! How would they survive an emergency job loss or injury?

The honest truth is that they wouldn't and most of the time they don't ever think something like that will happen. Then when it does, they'll be scrambling to collect the next unemployment check and have to go to bed thinking if they'll be in a cardboard mansion the next day. Don't be that statistic.

Tonight make sure you have a plan B ready just in case plan A doesn't work out. Think about where your money is for a rainy day. What is your emergency plan? Having a plan B doesn't mean you don't hope for the best or aren't optimistic…it just means you're PREPARED for the worst!

DAY 27 Completed: ____/____/_____

Write down your plan in the event of a financial emergency?

What can you do today to start prepping for the worst case scenario?

How are you going to ensure that you are always prepared for the worst in the future?

What did this mean to you?

"There's no harm in hoping for the best as long as you're prepared for the worst"

- Stephen King

DAY 28

- ALONE TIME IS MORE THAN JUST A SPA DAY -

Crawling into my apartment after ten days in Europe was bittersweet. I was stoked to shower in something that wasn't a 2 x 2 box, and I had grown a pretty sweet beard (more like a homeless stubble). The only real bitter part about coming back home was just the fact that I had to leave! What really made an impact was how I felt. I have been self-sufficient for a long time, surviving on my own paycheck, but nothing prepared me to travel a foreign country on my own and the feeling that resided with me afterward.

I had prepared for the trip for more than six months and was going to do the first leg with one of my best friends, Brock. We did London for two days and then Pamplona together for San Fermin or, as we call it, the running of the bulls. We separated after running with the bulls, and I handled Rome and Switzerland on my own. I got plenty of opportunities to meet new people and still stay connected with them, but the best part about the trip was the alone time I had in Rome, Pompeii and Switzerland. Sounds a little loner-esque, but I can assure you alone time isn't just for introverts.

After the tours I signed up for were over or early in the morning, I had a chance to get a cup of coffee on my own, walk the streets with no direction, and just get lost in a city with so much history. I spent time thinking of where I want to be in the future, what I wish to do with my life, who I love the most, and even had moments where my mind was BLANK. If you know me, you see it's a challenge for me to sit still, let alone stop thinking. I soaked in anything that crossed my mind and held on to the thought before I moved on to the next random one. I didn't have to think of anyone but myself for four days.

It is not selfish to understand everyone needs a little "me" time. This trip reminded me that I am my own person and can be secure in my presence. It allowed me to understand no matter how outgoing, extroverted, excitable, or whatever other adjective you possibly could think of, you need time on your own to just "reset." It allows you time to collect your thoughts, focus on your goals, and just pay attention to yourself. There isn't work involved; you're not getting phone calls, and the only person around is you, yourself, and your mind.

Psychologist K. Anders Ericsson of Florida State University has spent more than 30 years studying how people achieve the highest levels of expertise. Based not only on his personal research but also the review of other related studies, he concluded that most people could push themselves beyond their current limits for only an hour without rest. That's an hour straight driving our mind and body outside one's comfort zone. Ericsson exclaims, "Unless the daily levels of practice are restricted, such that subsequent rest and nighttime sleep allow the individuals to restore their equilibrium, individuals often encounter overtraining injuries and, eventually, incapacitating 'burnout.'

Although this particular study focused on avoiding burnout and overtraining injuries, it is the same idea. We need time to "reset" from all the stimulation we experience during the day, and being alone is the easiest way to do that.

SO WHAT DOES THIS MEAN TO YOU?

The majority of people in this world are more scared of being alone than spending time with the wrong people. I could tell just by the way people responded when they found out I spent time by myself overseas. "Weren't you lonely?!" was a common question and one I got excellent at answering.

You know these people. This could be the boyfriend/girlfriend hopper, the person that always needs to be with SOMEONE, or that guy always on social media. It happens to all of us at one point in time. Then you have a moment, a trip, an experience where the "alone" happens. You are by yourself with you and your thoughts. When you come out unscathed, mentally and physically, you realize that the time spent on your own only made you stronger. It turns someone into a person who settles for someone to love them into an individual who loves themselves.

If you are one of the people who is desperately afraid of being alone, I challenge you to try it. It doesn't need to be a trip overseas, but just some time to yourself, in your head, on a more frequent basis. An amazing book, *The Miracle Morning,* discusses something like this, which could include some absolute silence into your morning! If you think you are not one of those people and can handle "alone" time, then congratulations…test your theory. Go on a trip by yourself; explore the city you live in on your own, just do something by yourself.

It won't change the fact that we all desire companionship and I'm not saying that the human need for connection is bad. I think that companionship is an important part of our lives and as humans we crave (and NEED) those connections. What I am saying is that when we want the relationship with others, we commonly forget to stay connected with our internal desires and needs. Escape the extremely connected world for a while and see what it does for you.

DAY 28 Completed: ___/___/____

When was the last time you were truly alone? What was it like?

How can you turn your next bit of "alone" time into a time to self-reflect and grow?

How can you incorporate some personal time into each week?

What did this mean to you?

"If you want to soar in life, you must first learn to F.L.Y. (First Love Yourself)"

- Mark Sterling

DAY 29

- TAKE CONTROL OF YOUR SHIP... YOU'RE THE CAPTAIN -

Today is your day. You've made it through nearly 30 days of experiences, expanding your comfort zone, and creating a better you. By now you're comfortable with being uncomfortable and have caught on to the task of keeping your senses open to the lessons life has for you. Today keep an eye, ear, or your mind open to your own lesson. Something that life brings to you in the form of your daily life and share it here.

DAY 29 Completed: ____/____/_____

How many 'lessons' did you see today?

Did you notice more opportunities today because you were consciously looking or has it be trained?

How are you going to continue to do this when you close this book?

What did this mean to you?

> *"Give a Man a Fish you feed him for a day. Teach a man to fish and you feed him for a lifetime."*
>
> *– Chinese Proverb*

DAY 30

- DREAMS DON'T HAVE AN EXPIRATION DATE -

This isn't one of my stories. It's not a quote that someone pounded into my brain. It's something I learned on my own. By writing this book, investing in my future, and just growing up, I've found that dreams don't have an expiration date. Yes, things have happened in a different order than I expected, but looking back I wouldn't change a thing. The only thing holding you back from what you want is the person staring you back in the mirror. Don't let them tell you that you can't do what you want.

People don't remember what you did or how much money you'd made during your lifetime. That all fades with time. What stays with generations is the impact you made on them! The way you made the feel!

If you haven't noticed by now, this book was all about making you step outside of your comfort zone, providing a daily challenge to better yourself, and making you feel something you had not before. I hope by the time you've closed this book, you can look back over this past month and say this book made you do something that scared you, impacted your life in some way, and has honestly started each day the right way this month.

If this book inspires just one person to follow one of their dreams, learn something new, or simply take a vested interest in their own personal development, then I could die a happy (and way too young) man. Can you just fathom the idea of everyone in this world making a serious commitment in developing themselves?! All beauty pageant contestants would have to stop wishing for world peace because we might just have it.

Seriously though, we really have only one major road block in this life and it just happens to be attached at our shoulders. The way we feel, think, and our mental state can make or break us. There are natural disasters, sickness, health, free will, and billions of other things we as human beings cannot control. It doesn't matter how hard we try; life will take its natural course. So in that case, what can we do to have any kind of control?!

Attitude and effort.

That means you can only control the way you FEEL on a daily basis. YOU and your feelings control whether or not you're positive or negative that day. Have you ever turned your attitude around mid-day? If you think about it, an internal feeling changed your attitude and, in turn, your day. Don't believe me? Why do you think *The Secret* is such a successful book and lifestyle adjustment? Because it works and it proves your mental power is stronger than you think.

What about effort? YOU control how hard you work and push to do whatever you do on a regular basis. How many motivational stories end with a person lacking effort and a preserving attitude? That's right…zero. These two things are the most solid things we have as human beings that we DO have control of! When you have little under your control, you better make sure you capitalize on the things you can control…

The only constant in life is change and only you can control your attitude and effort towards it. Remember this the next time you've hit some speed bumps in your life and are just struggling. Keep pushing forward and remember only you can control your attitude and effort!

So with that said, a whole month of breaking out of your comfort zone, think about this hard…

What kind of legacy are you going to leave on this Earth? What is going to make you happy, healthy, and wealthy?

What does leaving a "legacy" with your name on it mean to you?

"I've learned that people will forget what you said, people will forget what you did, but people will never forget how you made them feel."

— Maya Angelou

WHAT THE FUTURE MEANS TO YOU…

The majority of this book addresses lessons we need to personally take on and GROW. A lot of my personal development has come from reading books that discuss things I mentioned earlier: everything from financial literacy and setting realistic goals to keeping a positive mental state and finding what truly motivates you. With that said, I have a favor to ask. If this book impacted you at all, I ask that you share it. You can pass along your copy or just get someone else a copy.

I also know this book is just one piece to the puzzle. Many of the lessons I've learned, I've accelerated the progression with numerous books and other resources. *Books like The Miracle Morning by Hal Elrod and People Buy You by Jeb Blount.* Websites like www.biggerpockets.com helped me get a better understanding of real estate.

If you'd like a full list of these resources, visit my website at www.joshcalcanis.com under resources.

Josh Calcanis
AUTHOR

Josh Calcanis wants to live in a world filled with diets that involve a moderate amount of Ben & Jerry's, motorcycles as the primary form of transportation, and the requirement to do something everyday that scares you.

As a sales professional, real estate investor, writer, and adrenaline junkie, Josh has successfully grown business as a sales professional in multiple scenarios and used the time outside of his career to build on his dreams. This everyday neighborhood guy from Florida has profitably invested in real estate, the stock market, other investment vehicles that so many people have access to. He is a passionate believer in not accepting what life gives you as a certainty, but more as a challenge and life lesson to step outside your comfort zone and create your own future.

When he isn't taking notes on the lessons he learned throughout the day, you can find him on his motorcycle, enjoying the outdoors, or with his family and friends.

MERAKI HOUSE
PUBLISHING

*Publishing with
Soul, Creativity & Love*

Meraki House Publishing, founded in 2015 has established its brand as an independent virtual publishing house designed to suit your needs as the Author, delivering the highest quality design, writing and editorial, publishing and marketing services to ensure your success.

"Where your needs as an Author have become ours as an independent Publishing House."

WWW.MERAKIHOUSE.COM

In partnership with
www.designisreborn.com

Copyright 2016, Meraki House Publishing

Marnie Kay, Founder & CEO
marniekay.com

www.ingramcontent.com/pod-product-compliance
Lightning Source LLC
Chambersburg PA
CBHW050531300426
44113CB00012B/2036